Today Is Mine

Brownlow Publishing Company, Inc.
6309 Airport Freeway, Fort Worth, Texas 76117

THIS BOOK BELONGS TO

_____

_____

_____19_____

Today Is Mine

365 daily devotions,
inspirational quotes, and
thought-provoking scriptures
for mastering the art of living.

Leroy Brownlow

Other Brownlow Gift Books

FOREWORD

Herein is my philosophy, presented in 365 brief essays, expressed in simple language, supported by the cherished words of the most renowned authors, philosophers, scholars and statesmen of all ages, plus quotations from the Bible.

It is obvious from the many quotations which bear on the topics that this volume is more than one man's view of life, that it is actually the tried and tested views of man through the centuries; and this is not surprising, for the true principles of successful living are not new. As Cicero said, "Nothing quite new is perfect." Truth is always truth, no matter when and how and by whom it is expressed.

It is my belief that these basic principles of life will help to give each day to the person who ponders them; and just as these reflections have pointed and inspired me to happier and fuller days, the hope is now entertained that they will help others.

LEROY BROWNLOW

RESOLUTIONS

I am resolved:

— To forget past mistakes and press on to greater achievements.
— To put first things first.
— To make my work a joy.
— To allow nothing to disturb my peace of mind.
— To never lose self-control.
— To spend so much time improving myself that I have no time for criticism of others.
— To think the best, work for it and expect it.
— To be a friend to man.
— To stand for the right.
— To be true.
— To be kind.
— To take every disappointment as a stimulant.
— To live on the sunny side of every cloud.
— To smile.
— To look ahead.
— To keep moving.

Resolve to perform what you ought; perform without fail what you resolve.

—Benjamin Franklin
1706 - 1790

I am resolved **what** to do . . . — Luke 16:4

PRAYER AT THE NEW YEAR

And these thoughts I pray: May I make every day mine, not waste a one; look forward, not backward. Grant me a life of peace, free from strife, animosity, resentment and retaliation. Help me to be a friend to all people, even to those who dislike me, manifesting more tolerance. May I be quick to see my own faults, and even quicker to correct them. Endue me with a gentle, kind and helpful spirit. May I abhor the evil, cleave to the good. Give me strength to be a man. Help me to count the cost and to pay the fare. May I walk with Thee — unto the end !

'Tis Heaven alone that is given away;
'Tis only God may be had for the asking.

—*James Russell Lowell*
1819 - 1891

Therefore hath thy servant found in his heart to pray this prayer unto thee. — II Samuel 7:27

PROGRESS IS MAN'S DISTINCTION

After a silver-haired visitor with mellow manners had left the home of friends, a young daughter, greatly impressed, commented to her mother: "Oh, if I could be an old lady like that, so sweet, serene, lovable and beautiful, I wouldn't mind being old."

The brilliant and discerning mother replied: "Remember — that kind of humanity was not grown in a hurry. It took her a long time to make her what she is. And if you are going to be that kind of an old lady, if you are going to paint yourself to be a portrait like that, you had better start mixing the colors and brushing a few strokes now."

> *Progress, man's distinctive mark alone,*
> *Not God's, and not the beasts': God is, they are;*
> *Man partly is, and wholly hopes to be.*

> —*Robert Browning*
> 1812 - 1889

. . . let us go on unto perfection. — Hebrews 6:1

EACH MAKES HIS WORLD

The world is a lot of things to a lot of people: generally, what each makes it, a beautiful and beneficial world to those who dig out its beauty and blessings. The good find good, and the evil find evil. For, in the last analysis the world is a mirror which reflects the little world each is.

There is such a thing as good luck, but only in sparing uncertainties. The more certain rule is: God blesses him who blesses himself. The tree grows the lumber, but not the house. Food feeds the body, but doesn't make the man; that he must do for himself — with God's help.

No man ever wetted clay and then left it, as if there would be bricks by chance and fortune.

—Plutarch
46 - 120

Whoso is wise, and will observe these things, even they shall understand the loving-kindness of the Lord.—Psalms 107:43

YOU — NOT ANCESTORS

You are neither a born winner nor a born loser. The way you play the game determines that.

It's your general behavior — not your genealogy — that adds the points. It's not the blue blood your parents gave you — but the briny sweat you give — that runs up the score. It's not who your forefathers were — but what you are — that makes the difference.

This generation won't let you hang onto your ancestors' coat tails; neither will it deny you a coat because they didn't have one. But you will have to earn it.

> *They will ask you, "What have you done?*
> *Not, "Who are your ancestors?"*
> *The famous veil in the sanctuary*
> *Is not reverenced by the faithful*
> *Because it came from the silkworm.*
>
> *—Saasi, the Persian poet*

The son shall not bear the iniquity of the father, neither shall the father bear the iniquity of the son: the righteousness of the righteous shall be upon him, and the wickedness of the wicked shall be upon him.—Ezekiel 18:20

MOMENTARY DUTY

In a **McGuffey's Reader** there is a story of an old clock that suddenly quit running. The reason: the clock counted the number of times it would have to tick in one year — 31,536,000 times. This was just too many ticks for a weary clock; so it lost its morale and stopped. Later it was explained to the clock all that was expected of it was to tick just one tick at a time. With this reflection, it regained its spirit and began running again.

So it is with man. Trying to live life in the lump is frightening. All that is necessary is to do your duty momentarily.

> *Fortune is like the market, where many times,*
> *if you can stay a little, the price will fall.*
>
> —*Francis Bacon*
> 1561 - 1626

They shall run, and not be weary; and they shall walk, and not faint.—Isaiah 40:31

AN IDEAL GOAL

Each person should have this goal: *May I become wiser, better and happier.* All other accomplishments are empty and vain. No matter what you have acquired — wealth, education, prestige — ask yourself: Am I wiser? Am I better? Am I happier?

If not, look for the cause in your own heart. Probably you will find that you need to develop more self-control and less irritation; more deliberation and less impulsiveness; more faith and less doubt. It is largely an internal problem. For out of the heart are the issues which determine the state of man.

Man is the artificer of his own happiness.

—Henry David Thoreau
1817 - 1862

I thought on my ways, and turned my feet unto thy testimonies.—Psalms 119:59

THOUGH YOU BEGIN SMALL

Fret not at small beginnings. The oak began as an acorn. The beautiful rainbow had its beginning in a drop of rain and a ray of light. The oozing through of one drop of water started the proverbial break in the dike. The muscular athlete once had trouble crawling. The university graduate started in the first grade. The massive international oil industry began with a little shallow well. Today's aviation can be traced back to a most humble beginning. A cent is the beginning of a dollar—ninety-nine more to go; it's little and cheap, but very religious — goes to church oftener than the dollar.

By viewing Nature, Nature's handmaid Art,
Makes mighty things from small beginnings grow.

—*John Dryden*
1631 - 1700

Though thy beginning was small, yet thy latter end should greatly increase.—Job 8:7

DO A GOOD JOB

The artificer requires more time, but his work is more valuable. It is not how much we do, but how well we do it that determines worth. The first measurement of any work is quality. Skill is power, a power which belongs to talent, devotion and patience. It adds stature to life. Monuments are erected to artists — not to bunglers.

Why rush to get out a slipshod job just to pursue more shoddiness in shoddy living? For no man's life is above his work. Haste makes waste, not only of the product, but of the life that turns it out.

> *But the great Master said, "I see*
> *No best in kind, but in degree;*
> *I gave a various gift to each,*
> *To charm, to strengthen, and to teach."*
>
> —*Henry Wadsworth Longfellow*
> 1807 - 1882

> Even to the artificers and builders gave they it, to buy hewn stone, and timber for couplings, and to floor the houses . . . And the men did the work faithfully.
> —II Chronicles 34:11, 12

WORLD IMPROVEMENT BEGINS WITH ME

World improvement is everybody's business. A person's very presence in the world bespeaks his being a responsible part of it; and that part, good or bad, must of necessity make the world a little better or a little worse.

So—just as you can improve the whole by improving the parts — world improvement must begin with me; and as I succeed in bettering self, I restore the world; for each evil conquered by me is that much of it put down in the world. A few broken habits will make the world more habitable.

I am to bless the world through what I am.

—*William Makepeace Thackeray*
1811 - 1863

For none of us liveth to himself, and no man dieth to himself.—Romans 14:7

CHANCE OR MISCHANCE — GRAB IT

No matter which way the ball bounces, it's your game. Play it to win. Yield not to misfortune. We have seen a wrong bounce, a fumbled ball taken for a touchdown on the athletic field—and in the game of life.

Misfortune is real. So is fortune. And on the law of averages there should be enough fortune to more than offset misfortune. But it is not always proportioned that way among all people. The reason — the human factor is more important than the ball's bounce. Fortune comes to those who grab chance and use it, and to those who take mischance and triumph over it. Others it flees.

Yield not thy neck
To fortune's yoke, but let thy dauntless mind
Still ride in triumph over all mischance.

—*William Shakespeare*
1564 - 1616

We went through fire and through water: but thou broughtest us out into a wealthy place.
—Psalms 66:12

LEARNING FROM EXPERIENCE

All men make mistakes, but all wise men are less apt to make them the second time. Though man is human enough to err, one hope for him is his being divine enough to regret it; this means he still has a chance.

In spite of all of man's boners, one thing in his favor is the ability to learn from them. And to learn from blunders is a most practical accomplishment. We make enough errors to get educated, if we acquire knowledge from them. Through this process, fallible man can have a brighter expectation tomorrow. This is reason enough for living!

If life had a second edition, how I would correct the proofs.
　　　　　　　　　　　—*Percy Bysshe Shelley*
　　　　　　　　　　　1792 - 1822

For I have learned by experience.—Genesis 30:27

BE ADAPTABLE

Our world is one of thorns and thistles as well as roses and violets. Practicality demands that we adjust ourselves to both. We can't always have everything just like we want it. Flexibility is required. Each must do the best he can. And when thorns prick, we find helpfulness in scenting the perfume with the resolution to be more watchful next time.

Some things about life can be changed to our liking — others can't; and if they can't, then we must change ourselves just to live. This is the art of living — adjustment and readjustment — and it is accomplished by self.

> *The grass must bend when the wind blows across it.*
>
> *—Confucius*
> 551 - 479 B.C.

> I would hasten my escape from the windy storm and tempest.—Psalms 55:8

HELP EACH OTHER

"Help! Help me!" These are the words we hear from every nook and corner of the earth. For mankind is in trouble; he hurts; he has needs.

If you can relieve a need, you will always be in demand. Humanity's beaten paths invariably lead to the doors of the helpful.

It is a law of nature that there be reciprocal help. It is too human to be ignored. It is too necessary not to be followed.

Accordingly, let us render kindness for the same reason a flower blooms — we were made for that purpose.

I know no great men except those who have rendered service to the human race.

—*Francois Marie Arouet Voltaire*
1694 - 1778

They helped every one his neighbor; and every one said to his brother, Be of good courage.—Isaiah 41:6

HEARING EAR AND SEEING EYE

Ears that hear and eyes that see. Great assets. And somewhat uncommon. With them, one can see and observe, hear and perceive. He can get the message of heaven and earth. "The heavens declare the glory of God."

The "tongues in trees" whisper to him that they are known by their fruits. The "books in running brooks" teach him that nature seeks its own level. The "sermons in stones" point up the need of hewing.

He can see good in every thing: even in adversity, which invites humility, self-examination, adjustment, initiative. He is not fooled by hardship's disguise.

Sweet are the uses of adversity;
Which, like the toad, ugly and venomous,
Wears yet a precious jewel in his head;
And this our life, exempt from public haunt,
Finds tongues in trees, books in the running brooks,
Sermons in stones, and good in everything.

—William Shakespeare
1564 - 1616

The hearing ear, and the seeing eye, the Lord hath made even both of them.—Proverbs 20:12

THE LOCAL JURY

Conscience is the jury in man's soul which sits in judgment of his conduct. Each case should be tried by the laws of God before the judiciary of man's own moral consciousness. When human behavior is tried in the court of divine laws and pronounced "not guilty" by the jury of conscience, it is then — and only then — that man is free.

No matter what a state or Federal tribunal may say, it's the local jury — deep down in the soul — that really frees or imprisons a man.

O conscience, let me be free and today shall be mine.

His gain is loss; for he that wrongs his friend
Wrongs himself more, and ever has about
A silent court and jury, and himself
The prisoner at the bar, ever condemned.

—*Alfred Tennyson*
1809 - 1892

...their conscience bearing witness therewith, and their thoughts one with another accusing or else excusing them.—Romans 2:15, A.S.V.

PRACTICE WHAT YOU ADVOCATE

One Sunday the brother of the minister, a physician, visited the church services. At the conclusion, a lady said to him, "Sir, do you preach, too?"

"No, my brother preaches; I practice," was the reply.

Whether you profess faith in religion, medicine or anything else, a living demonstration of your advocacy will speak louder than anything you say.

It is not amiss, therefore, for us to say, "Preacher, live your sermon; physician, take your medicine." Then we shall listen!

Practice is the best of all instructors.

—Publius Syrus
1st Century B. C.

And how I kept back nothing that was profitable unto you, but have showed you and have taught you.—Acts 20:20

RIGHT

Right is the measure of civilization's progress. Every step of progress has been from right to right; and every retrogression has been from wrong to wrong. Right is the solution to the problem; wrong is the problem.

Switching their appearances changes nothing. Reclothing wrong only primps it in new apparel. Sweeping it under the rug only hides it in deception.

But right does not tolerate wrong, dress it as you please or cover it as you will. Right centers on something worthier than semblance — principles not presentation. Right has its built-in rewards, and so does wrong its curses — a dagger up its sleeve.

Fools make a mock at sin, will not believe
It carries such a dagger in its sleeve.

—*William Shakespeare*
1564 - 1616

And thou shalt do that which is right and good in the sight of the Lord; that it may be well with thee.—Deuteronomy 6:18

LOVE WINS

Love is the winning quality. It wins when everything else fails. You can't win many people by knocking them, nor by fussing with them, nor by embarrassing them, nor by exploiting them, nor by threatening them, nor by freezing them; but you can thaw them and draw them by simply loving them.

Love wins when politics, reason and fear fail. The discerning do not want political treatment. Reason often meets a complete rejection. Fear is apt to answer blow for blow. But love finds hearts receptive; for they see no reason to be wary, feel no need to argue and sense no cause to be afraid.

Love is the sun against whose melting beams the winter cannot stand. There is not one human being in a million whose clay heart is hardened against love.

—Henry Allen Tupper

We love him, because he first loved us.
—I John 4:19

RULE YOURSELF

By ruling yourself you can be a king. More than a king! For he who governs his own life, controls his passions and fears; he reigns in a dominion where kings have often failed.

Losing self-control will enslave a man in naughtiness, add to his nervous troubles, multiply his strife, mar his reputation, drive off his friends, erase the smile from his children's faces and take from him his self-respect. You know you don't want that to happen, so keep a tight rein on yourself. For you must either be a king in your own kingdom or a slave in another's.

The most important thing is to learn to rule oneself.

—Johann Wolfgang von Goethe
1749 - 1832

He that is slow to anger is better than the mighty; and he that ruleth his spirit than he that taketh a city.—**Proverbs 16:32**

EVERY AGE IS SUITABLE

Every age is too rewarding to be wasted. The plan of life is just right: childhood, youth, middle age, old age. Everything comes to us just when we are ready to receive it. To have an age precipitated upon us before we are ready or withheld from us after we are would be most disastrous. Each age has its own peak, and as you get older you can see life from a higher vantage.

Many are too much disposed to renown the past, renege the present, and reanimate the future before it arrives. Live now. It's the only age you have.

Strike when thou wilt, the hour of rest,
But let my last days be my best.

—*Robert Browning*
1812 - 1889

If they obey and serve him, they shall spend their days in prosperity, and their years in pleasures.—Job 36:11

ASPIRATIONS

The supreme incentive to lofty achievement is high objectives. The driving power of an aspiration has lifted many a lowly person. And those who rose were worthy of the elevation for they tried. Their purpose and accomplishments reflect their merit, especially when viewed in the light of noble motives.

Each has the wings to rise, but not every one has the mind to lift them. Man can soar only on aspiring wings that beat, and when they do, his sky knows no limits. What is needed is an aspiration that is not content to be grounded — nor to fly too low.

> *Lord, let me not be content*
> *With life in trifling service spent —*
> *Make me aspire!*
>
> *—Anonymous*

Know ye not that they which run in a race run all, but one receiveth the prize? So run, that ye may obtain.—I Corinthians 9:24

COURTESY — THE UNIVERSAL LANGUAGE

If a courteous word or two will make a man feel good, then only a knave will fail to give it to him.

Courtesy is thoughtfulness oozing from an unselfish heart.

Courtesy will make you liked. It casts a spell as it manifests little acts of attention and consideration, giving others the preference while eating, sitting, standing, walking, in the shop, in the office and at play.

Courtesy is the passport to the world. It is the universal language. Speak it and the world listens. It makes you welcome. Like oil to machinery, it keeps associations running smoothly.

And it doesn't cost a cent!

How sweet and gracious, even in common speech,
Is that fine sense which men call Courtesy!
It transmutes aliens into trusting friends,
And gives its owner passport round the globe.

> —*James Thomas Fields*
> 1816 - 1881

...love as brethren, be pitiful, be courteous.
—I Peter 3:8

BE CONTENT

Avoid discontent and fret. There is a time to weep and a time to rejoice, but there is no time for a place between the two called discontent.

To the malcontent no house is comfortable, no clothes satisfactory, no job rewarding, no day happy.

The discontented person should ask: "With whom would I swap places, a complete swap, all or none?"

Why waste your energy, time and health to no avail? Contentment will conserve your strength and turn your mind loose to think constructively. But discontent — what a waste!

Peace comes from enjoying what you have and by losing the desire for what you can't have.

> *When Fuss and Fret was all my fare*
> *It got no grounds, as I could see,*
> *So when away my caring went*
> *I counted cost and was content.*
>
> —*John Bryom*
> 1692 - 1763

And be content with such things as ye have.—Hebrews 13:5

WHEN ONE IS LOYAL

One sinew of character that compensates for a whole lot of weakness is loyalty. Husband and wife demand it, and without it marriage fails. Business success requires it, and devoid of it bankruptcy approaches. National survival necessitates it, and without it doom draws near.

Loyalty is an iron chain of many strong links: love, bravery, self-sacrifice, honesty, truthfulness, steadfastness.

Loyalty is convinced that anything worth obtaining — husband, wife, friend, or any association — is worth retaining and thus is unwavering in its fidelity to the same. Loyalty protects, for it is unafraid. Loyalty perseveres, for it has grit. It's the unfailing spirit that stands the test. It's no traitor!

His words are bonds; his oaths are oracles; his heart is as far from fraud as heaven from earth.

—*William Shakespeare*
1564 - 1616

... but showing all good fidelity.—Titus 2:10

HONESTY IS MORE THAN POLICY

"Honesty's the best policy," so declared Miguel de Cervantes who lived from 1547 to 1616. But honesty is more than policy, more than prudence, more than procedure based primarily on material interest.

While honesty will deal you a better hand in all the affairs of life, it is not played just for gain. It is a principle that is adhered to for honesty's sake because it is right. Doing the honest thing is something the honest person does because he is honest; to be dishonest would be out of character. He's honest, win or lose!

I am not bound to win, but
I am bound to be true.
I am not bound to succeed, but
I am bound to live up to what light I have.

—Abraham Lincoln
1809 - 1865

Thou shalt not have in thy bag divers weights, a great and a small. Thou shalt not have in thine house divers measures, a great and a small.—Deuteronomy 25:13,14

LITTLE LOWER THAN ANGELS

Man! What a unique creature! A little lower than the angels! So constituted that his possibilities are unlimited!

He is a whole library in one volume.
He is a complete garden hidden in one seed.

With more power than a king, he has dominion over the earth. He can call the plays, provided he stays within the rules of the game. He is the maker of his own destiny, lives where he chooses and how he chooses.

He is the only creature which rises by bowing, for he finds elevation in his subjection to his Maker.

> *What a piece of work is a man! how noble in reason! how infinite in faculty! in form and moving how express and admirable! in action how like an angel! in apprehension how like a god!*
>
> —*William Shakespeare*
> 1564 - 1616

> What is man, that thou art mindful of him? ... For thou hast made him a little lower than the angels, and hast crowned him with glory and honor.—Psalms 8:4, 5

DEVELOPED BEAUTY

It is better to develop good looks than to be born with them. The most adorable beauty does not wrinkle with the years, or wither at the touch of fever, like a drought-stricken flower, or lose its covering, like a frost-bitten tree. It is seen more clearly with examination. It is viewed more admiringly with time.

But Socrates called born beauty a short-lived tyranny; Theophrastus, a silent-cheat; Theocritus, a delightful prejudice; Plato, a privilege of nature; Homer, a glorious gift of nature; and Ovid, a favor bestowed by the gods.

We can add one thing sure—outward beauty deserves no praise unless matched with the inward charm of self-development.

Good nature is more agreeable in conversation than wit, and gives a certain air to the countenance which is more amiable than beauty.

—*Joseph Addison*
1672 - 1719

As a jewel of gold in a swine's snout, so is a fair woman which is without discretion.
—Proverbs 11:22

MEDITATE SOME

Everyone needs to steal away for a little while each day to the loneliness of meditation. It gets you off the treadmill of superficial living. It shuts out the noise from the grind of the world and lets you hear the voice that speaks out of silence.

No great work has ever been accomplished without pondering. The world's greats have always sought solitude for musing.

It has been said that Leonardo de Vinci, the renowned artist, would sit almost motionless for days at a time meditating and getting the inspiration for his masterpieces. In musing he nursed his thoughts and it paid off in greatness.

> *By all means, use some time to be alone;*
> *Salute thyself — see what thy soul doth wear;*
> *Dare to look in thy chest, for 'tis thine own,*
> *And tumble up and down what thou findest there.*

> —*William Wordsworth*
> 1770 - 1850

Let the words of my mouth, and the meditation of my heart, be acceptable in thy sight, O Lord, my strength, and my redeemer.—Psalms 19:14

READ THE BIBLE

Should I read the Bible? Yes! But more importantly I should let it read me. Its philosophies are profoundest. Its counsels are wisest. Its inspirations are loftiest. Its consolations are sweetest. Its goals are highest. Its rebukes are sharpest.

Unopened, the Bible will never read me — nor feed me; but when pored over, it will do both. It will glorify the mind, guard the heart, lift the eye, strengthen the hand and guide the feet.

Yes! I should read it to be smart and follow it to be smarter. For of all the Bible versions, the best translation is the one put into action.

From the time that at my mother's feet or my father's knee, I learned to lisp verses from the sacred writings, they have been my daily study and vigilant contemplation.

—Daniel Webster
1782 - 1852

The entrance of thy words giveth light.
—Psalms 119:130

AS GOES SELF-RELIANCE

He who has lost self-reliance has lost all. Without it there is no inspiration; devoid of it there is no courage; free of it there is no concerted effort.

Doubt whom you will, but not God or yourself. They are the two upon whom you must rely the most. Hardly one man in a hundred knows what he can do for himself — with God's help. If the worst should come to worst—if all other assistance should fail — you and He can still make a go of it.

As goes your self-dependence, so goes yourself — up or down.

To character and success, two things, contradictory as they may seem, must go together — humble dependence and manly independence: humble dependence on God and manly reliance on self.

—*William Wordsworth*
1770 - 1850

The God of heaven, he will prosper us; therefore we his servants will arise and build.—Nehemiah 2:20

THE BEST IS UP TO YOU

Having the best in life depends upon you:

— The best thought: you're the offspring of God.
— The best book: your Bible read.
— The best sermon: the one your good life preaches.
— The best quality: love you give and love you receive.
— The best play: work you enjoy.
— The best cheerfulness: sunniness you scatter.
— The best peace: inside you.
— The best teacher: your mistakes.
— The best way out: the opening you make.
— The best gratification: the knowledge you have done your work well.
— The best day: the one you make.

The story's about you.

—Horace
65 - 8 B.C.

Is not my help in me?—Job 6:13

THE PESSI*MIST* IT

The pessimist is a loser every way you figure it. He is not mentally prepared to cash in on good things. To him every hill is a mountain, every river is uncrossable, and every star is ready to fall. He walks in shadows when the sun is shining; he hears thunder when there isn't a cloud in sight; and he sips lightly from his glass, thinking the well is going to run dry.

A merchant of gloom, that describes him, but his customers are few. Frankly, I prefer to put my money on the optimist.

> *He growled at morning, noon, and night,*
>   *And trouble sought to borrow;*
> *Although today the sky was bright,*
>   *He knew 'twould storm tomorrow;*
> *A thought of joy he could not stand,*
>   *And struggled to resist it;*
> *Though sunshine dappled all the land*
>   *This sorry pessimist it.*
>
>   —*Nixon Waterman*

For as he thinketh in his heart, so is he.—Proverbs 23:7

DO WHAT YOU CAN

In a roaring and flashing thunderstorm, a family gathered into what they thought was the safest room. They huddled in fear. One of them was a little girl who folded her hands, closed her eyes and prayed. Then she confidently said, "O mamma, I have done what I could."

Oh! how it would add to life if we could say, *I have done what I could.*

The satisfaction would be most gratifying. Many a person, after living up to some strenuous duty, has been heard to say, "Thank God! I have done my part."

That is the way to climb. The ladder is duty.

Were it not wisdom, then, to close our eyes
On duties crowding only to appal?
No; duty is our ladder to the skies,
And, climbing not, we fall.

—*Robert Leighton*
1611 - 1684

She hath done what she could.—Mark 14:8

OVERCAUTION DOES NOTHING

Success climbs its ladder cautiously, but over-caution never gets off the ground. He who is so wary that he is afraid to try for fear he will fail has already failed.

Overcaution is too much of a good thing, just like no caution is too much of a bad thing. Stop all risks and you stop the world: the sailing of ships, the drilling for oil, the sowing of seeds and the harvesting of crops.

The good life has its hazards; and blessed is he who lives it circumspectly — but lives it!

Who waits until the wind shall silent keep
Will never find the ready hour to sow;
Who watcheth clouds will have no time to reap.

—H. H. Jackson

He that observeth the wind shall not sow;
and he that regardeth the clouds shall not reap.
—Ecclesiastes 11:4

MONEY IS WHAT YOU MAKE IT

One of the strongest influences in this world is the love of money. Shouldn't be, but is. Yet money within itself is not bad. It is rather good, but it's the bad people who cause it to take on the appearance of themselves.

Without doubt, man's attitude toward money contributes much to his happiness or sorrow, peace or discontent; for many of his blessings or curses center around it, depending on what he makes it — servant or master.

Dug from the mountainside, washed in the glen.
Servant am I, or the master of men;
  Steal me, I curse you,
  Earn me, I bless you,
Grasp me and hoard me, a fiend shall possess you.
  Lie for me, die for me,
  Covet me, take me.
Angel or devil, I am what you make me —
  MONEY !

                  —Anonymous

For the love of money is the root of all evil.—I Timothy 6:10

BE AGREEABLE

The bristly dog is not much for agreement. That's all right, but it's his disagreeable way of expressing it that repels us. We prefer the agreeable dog; he's not so beastly.

And our choices of people are no different — not that all have to conform to our views, but we do demand that they be agreeable.

The practical thought for me is: The world is filled with would-be friends I haven't won and never will by barking and biting. The behavior that wins them is affable and amiable, conversable and considerate — not frictional.

Animals are such agreeable friends.
They ask no questions; they pass no criticisms.

—*George Eliot*
1819 - 1880

Let every one of us please his neighbor
for his good to edification.—Romans 15:2

February 7

ECONOMY RAISES REVENUE

Your ship won't come in except through the Straits of Economy. You can increase your wealth by decreasing your wants. You can raise your wages by lowering your expenses. You can have more by wasting less. What you make is not as important as how you handle it.

This requires efficiency, planning and the maturity to stick with the plans. Economy does not mean no spending — it means wise spending. Frugality takes the view that a thing not needed is too high at any price. And there are so many things we don't need!

> *Economy is in itself a source of great revenue.*
> —*Lucius Annaeus Seneca*
> 8 B.C. - 65 A.D.

The younger son ... wasted his substance ... and he began to be in want.—Luke 15:13, 14

WHAT DO YOU SEE?

As a battle was being fought, a general said to a private, "Soldier, what do you see?"

"A lost battle, sir," was the reply.

The general responded, "Where you see failure, I see triumph."

It is amazing how much difference there is in what men see. Where one views a hamlet, another a city; where one beholds ugliness, another beauty; and where one sees defeat, another victory. The difference is in the men — not the things they behold. The sights are fairer to those with deeper insights. And backbone gives them special lenses?

> *I came, I saw, I conquered.*
>
> *—Julius Caesar*
> 100 - 44 B.C.

Eyes have they, but they see not.—Psalms 115:5

BENEFICIENCE

I can make today mine by being beneficent. To receive and receive and never give blights man, for it is a perversion of the flow of blessings. The earth gives to man and he in return must give to others to strike a noble balance, without which the hoarder suffers the greatest loss — the loss of self-respect, usefulness and happiness.

Your attitude toward giving — sharing — manifests your attitude toward life: toward yourself, your neighbor, and the Great Giver. Toward self the donor is unselfish; toward his neighbor he is sympathetic; and toward God he is grateful.

That man may last, but never lives,
Who much receives, but nothing gives;
Whom none can love, whom none can thank, —
Creation's blot, creation's blank.

—Thomas Gibbons

For I was ahungered, and ye gave me meat: I was thirsty, and ye gave me drink: I was a stranger and ye took me in.—Matthew 25:35

NO AFFECTATION

Be natural! The only way to be somebody is to be yourself. Trying to wear another's personality — look and act like him — is as unnatural as trying to wear his teeth, and just as nauseating. A comical, obnoxious sham! And what the pretender doesn't know is, his imitation personality is nearly as hard to sell as false faces would be to angels.

In the drama of life you are cast in only one role — yourself — and you should play it, not imitate another. This does not bar improvements, but make them as the real man you are.

Be yourself, and be the person you hope to be.

—Robert Louis Stevenson
1850 - 1894

Now therefore present yourselves before the Lord.—I Samuel 10:19

CAPITALIZE ON TALENT

If nature bestows varied talents on different people — and it does — then it is wise for a person to do the thing for which nature has best fitted him. This is why it is best for the donkey to bray and the bird to sing — each has that aptitude.

Success comes easier when you do what you were cut out to do. The world never looks empty to him who finds his place and fills it. Using your capability will make you more capable; but burying your talent will start a cemetery in your own life.

What one man does, another fails to do;
What's fit for me may not be fit for you.

—Anonymous

... to every man according to his several ability.—Matthew 25:15

WISE RULER

Abraham Lincoln's own words bespeak his greatness:

— His love for the common people: "God must be a lover of the common people, or he would not have made so many of them."
— His honesty: "If, in your judgment, you cannot be an honest lawyer, resolve to be honest without being a lawyer."
— His commitment to right: "I am not bound to win, but I am bound to be true. I am not bound to succeed, but I am bound to live up to what light I have."
— His compassion and foresight: "I believe this nation cannot endure permanently half slave and half free."
— His resolution: "... that we here highly resolve that these dead shall not have died in vain ..."
— His trust in God: "Without the assistance of the Divine Being ... I cannot succeed. With that assistance I cannot fail!"

Honest Abe.

—*Anonymous*

(Affectionately used by the people)

Look out a man discreet and wise, and set him over the land.—Genesis 41:33

LOOK AFTER HEALTH

Health is more valuable than wealth; without it, all people are poor. The world turns at such a fast pace an unhealthy body has trouble keeping up. Regrettable but true, the world has blessings the sickly person finds hard to enjoy.

So — next to spirituality — put health at the top of your priority list. For money is of little value to the person who has lost health. What's the point in having delicious food you can't eat? A luxury car in which you can't ride? Or a big house when you are confined to one room — a sick room?

Look to your health; if you have it, praise God, and value it next to a good conscience; for health is the second blessing that we mortals are capable of; a blessing that money cannot buy.

—*Izzak Walton*
1593 - 1683

Beloved, I wish above all things that thou mayest prosper and be in health, even as thy soul prospereth.—III John 2

WHAT LOVE FEELS

Love is the digitalis of the heart — the world's most powerful stimulant. It is the stimulus to climb mountains, swim rivers, wade snows, cross deserts, sleep in the cold, work in the heat, and through it all whisper, "You are my Valentine."

It is the slowest and quickest quality: Slowest to doubt — quickest to believe. Slowest to criticize — quickest to approve. Slowest to irritate — quickest to smile. Slowest to accuse — quickest to excuse.

Love is the whole world, but only for lovers.

I NEVER knew before, what such love as you made me feel, was; I did not believe in it; my Fanny was afraid of it, lest it should burn me up. But if you will fully love me, though there may be some fire 'twill not be more than we can bear when moistened and bedewed with Pleasures ... Ever yours my love.
(Written to Fanny Brawne)

—*John Keats*
1795 - 1821

And Jacob loved Rachel.—Genesis 29:18

CASTING OFF BURDENS

Burdens are not so burdensome when they are laid aside at night. It's bearing them day and night that kills. Not even a mule can hold up long at that. What we need is not lighter burdens so much as rested backs.

Practical living requires you to put away your bothers over night. The chances are most of them will look lighter in the morning; if not, you will be stronger to face them after a night's rest.

The camel, at the close of day,
Kneels down upon the sandy plain
To have his burden lifted off
And rest again.

My soul, thou too should to thy knees
When daylight draweth to a close,
And let thy Master lift the load
And grant repose.

—Anonymous

Cast thy burden upon the Lord, and he shall sustain thee.—Psalms 55:22

BAD COMPANY

An old parrot flew out of a farm house and joined some crows in a watermelon field. The farmer, not knowing this and wanting to protect the fruit of his labors, blasted them with his shotgun. The results were three dead crows and one ruffled parrot with a missing toe.

The farmer tenderly took him home where the excited children gathered around and asked, "What did it?"

"Bad company! Bad company!" answered the parrot.

He spoke wiser than he knew. His foolish choice of associates had endangered him.

So it is with man — bad days come from bad companions, and better days come from better associates.

> *'Tis better to be alone than in bad company.*
> —*George Washington*
> 1732 - 1799

He that walketh with wise men shall be wise: but a companion of fools shall be destroyed.—Proverbs 13:20

FAITHFUL IN SMALL MATTERS

Fidelity in small things is at the base of every **great** life. The way you handle the small things shows your character for the big things. Such **consequences** come from little causes, which maybe are not so little after all.

An old sailor expressed it: "A ship may be sunk by a cargo of sand, as well as by a cargo of mill-stones." In that event, the little grains of sand are not so little. Thus, the things that are thought to be little are big enough to float you or sink you.

> *In great matters men show themselves as they wish to be seen; in small matters, as they are.*
> —*Gamaliel Bradford*

> He that is faithful in that which is least is faithful also in much; and he that is unjust in the least is unjust also in much.
> —Luke 16:10

HAVING REQUIRES STRIVING

When I was a little boy someone in the family (which often meant me) had to do the churning. More valuable than the butter was the lesson that having requires doing, that very little comes to man except through exertion.

One reason we do not find more valuables is our inadequate search. We quit too soon. Our world has its good things, but ordinarily they are not on the surface nor in shallow water; obtaining them requires thought and sweat and patience. We can't have the butter without churning the milk, nor the kernel without husking the corn.

Long do we live upon the husks of corn,
While neath untasted lie the kernels still.

—Jones Very

He said unto Simon, Launch out into the deep, and let down your nets for a draught.
—Luke 5:4

HANDLING FORTUNE

Develop yourself on the inside until you are big enough to handle promotions and riches. If you are not big enough for good fortune, you will be better off if it never comes; for it has destructive and diverse effects on little people. It swells their heads and shrinks their hearts. It makes them rich but poor. While they have money to spend, it won't buy what they need.

But recovery is always in sight, for fortune won't go far unaccompanied by sense. Let's never forget — sense can outrun money any day.

It requires greater virtue to sustain good fortune than bad.
—*La Rochefoucauld*
1613 - 1680

There is that maketh himself rich yet hath nothing: there is that maketh himself poor, yet hath great riches.—Proverbs 13:7

WHY COMPARE YOURSELF?

Comparing your life with others is hurtful and useless, odious and foolish. If you match your life with inferiors, it brings a perverted satisfaction which means nothing; and if you liken it to superiors, it creates discontent by focusing attention on what you don't have.

Why compare? You wouldn't swap if you could; for it involves another's health, disposition, appetite, habits, friends, loves, hates, sorrows, interests — not just his talent or wealth. For you, success and happiness are found in being yourself and in living your own life in whatever state you are compelled to live it.

> *Let us then be up and doing,*
> *with a heart for any fate.*
>
> *—Henry Wadsworth Longfellow*
> 1807 - 1882

But they, measuring themselves by themselves, and comparing themselves among themselves, are not wise.—II Corinthians 10:12

LIVING FOR OTHERS

Others! The ones we love! What a motivating power for struggling on! And this is not lower-class, middle-class or upper-class morality. This is the force of love which is true wherever you find this age-old quality.

Loyalty to others won't let us quit. It causes men to search their souls for a little extra strength, which they find and which spurs them on to glorious victory in the face of seeming defeat. And this devotion which holds the welfare of others dearer than life will prompt them, if need be, to give the last heart-beat in their defense.

> *When all our hopes are gone,*
> *'Tis well our hands must still keep toiling on*
> *For others' sake.*
>
> —*Anonymous*

I will lay down my life for thy sake.
—John 13:37

WORTHY TO RULE

When a man treasures the rights of men — as Washington did; and prefers principle to profit — as Washington preferred; and believes "that man was not designed by the All-wise Creator to live for himself alone" — as Washington believed; and is courageous enough to stand up to opposition — as Washington stood; and towers above trickery and partisanship — as Washington towered; and refuses to be a king — as Washington refused; and trusts in "the All-wise Disposer of events" — as Washington trusted; and sees heroics in ragged men with a cause — as Washington saw — that man is truly worthy of rulership and a place "in the hearts of his countrymen."

The red coats do look best, but it takes the ragged boys to do the fighting.

—*George Washington*
1732 - 1799

Moreover thou shalt provide out of all the people able men, such as fear God, men of truth, hating covetousness; and place such over them, to be rulers.—Exodus 18:21

READ GOOD BOOKS

Reading is a brainy affair: you use your own and borrow the author's. It is a dual mental exercise whereby you increase your power by using and feeding your brain.

Speaking of power, most of man's is from his eyes up. Accordingly, a great opportunity to increase human force is in reading. The mightiness of good books is given to those who study them.

This is a must! For man cannot live by bread alone. His nature calls for progress. And a few moments of profound reading each day will give him the necessary stimulus and adjustment for his ascendancy.

He who loveth a book will never want a faithful friend, a wholesome counsellor, a cheerful companion, or an effectual comforter.

—*Isaac Barrow*

Give attendance to reading...
—I Timothy 4:13

LEARN AND LIVE

Live and learn, but more importantly, learn and live — that's my motto. Let's take the lessons in the right order: First, know yourself. Second, know what you ought to do. Third, know what is needed to make you do it.

All around us are contributory lessons to these three. There are teaching tongues in everybody: in the literate and illiterate, in the young and old, in friends and enemies. There are enlightening books in everything; in remembrance and forgetfulness, in happiness and sorrow, in harmony and discord, in thrift and waste, in trial and error, in victory and defeat. No question about the teachers. What about the students?

> *I grow old learning something new every day.*
> —*Salon*
> 638(?) - 559 B.C.

> Take fast hold of instruction; let her not go: keep her; for she is thy life.
> —Proverbs 4:13

ERR ONLY IN JUDGMENT

Every time the ball carrier takes the ball he runs the risk of fumbling. And in this game called life, you also run the risk of poor judgment every time you use it. But if you don't, you never will reach the goal line.

Mistakes being the common lot of man, you are sure to make some; however, you have humanity's sympathy, provided your heart is true. At times your judgment is sure to prove itself blind; but if that is the only mistake — judgment — and the world sees in you no baseness, it is apt to be rather tolerant. For the motive puts every error in a new perspective.

We are eager for the right;
O ye who lead, take heed!
Blindness we may forgive,
But baseness we will smite.

—William Vaughn Moody

But I obtained mercy, because I did it ignorantly...—I Timothy 1:13

THE VIRTUE IS IN TRYING

A person never fails if he really tries to succeed; though he does not reach the set goal, he reaches several rewards just for the trying.

Not all who dig for gold find it, but they do strengthen their muscles. The struggle is more valuable than the prize. Truly, man owes his well-being to that striving the world calls effort. While the struggle grips his attention and absorbs his interest, it adds to his regulations, enthusiasm, drive and contentment.

Consequently, if I maintain the forward pace, keeping my eye on the goal — come what may — I am sure to be a winner.

> *If what shone afar so grand*
> *Turns to nothing in thy hand,*
> *On again — the virtue lies*
> *In the struggle, not the prize.*
>
> *—Lord Houghton*
> 1809 - 1885

Let thine eyes look right on, and let thine eyelids look straight before thee.—Proverbs 4:25

QUIT? NEVER!

There is indescribable gratification in being able to say: "I have done it — this thing I sought to do — I have done it." It is a tribute to constancy, that stickability which carries us through our adversities and lifts us over our obstacles, even those which appear insurmountable.

Continuancy finally wins. If you are knocked down, don't give up — get up; and if you can't, crawl. It is all right to stop long enough to get your breath, but don't surrender. The victory goes not to the man who is the least hit, but to him who won't quit.

The heights by great men reached and kept
Were not attained by sudden flight,
But they, while their companions slept
Were toiling upward in the night.

—*Henry Wadsworth Longfellow*
1807 - 1882

And let us not be weary in well doing: for in due season we shall reap, if we faint not.
—Galatians 6:9

LET BYGONES BE BYGONES

Forget it! Ah! what power to rid your heart of anxiety and disquietude.

Some cruel deed has wounded you, forget it; don't think of it again.

An unprecipitated harsh or unjust sentence has irritated you, let it rest; the guilty one may have only given vent to some pent up nervousness, and will be pleased to see it forgotten.

Some unproved scandal is about to estrange you from an old friend, forget it and thus prove your charity and preserve your peace of mind.

A suspicious look threatens to cool your affection, forget it; better still, return it with a look of trust that restores confidence.

> *To be wronged is nothing unless you continue to remember it.*
>
> —*Confucious*
> 551 - 479 B.C.

...thou hast cast all my sins behind thy back.—Isaiah 38:17

LIFE AS SCHOOL

When we view life as a school, we can better pass the tests to which we are subjected, knowing that as we excel in each vicissitude we demonstrate more fitness to advance to a higher grade.

In some tests we don't make "A"; once in a while fail; but as long as we are in school — a lifetime — we still have an opportunity for improvement. Some of the lessons are hard to learn; but with the penalty for failing so bitter and the reward for passing so big, we usually wise up somewhat before school closes.

> *Lord, let me make this rule:*
> *To think of life as school,*
> *And try my best*
> *To stand each test,*
> *And do my work*
> *And nothing shirk.*
> —*Maltbie D. Babcock*

Or speak to the earth and it shall teach thee.—Job 12:8

SUCCESS FORMULIZED

Formula for success:

— Know yourself.
— Take time to think.
— Use good judgment.
— Make plans.
— Be optimistic — talk like a winner.
— Give yourself to your task.
— Learn to say *no*.
— Amend your faults.
— Get up when knocked down.
— Love God and man.

Nothing succeeds like success.

—Alexandre Dumas
1824 - 1895

The desire accomplished is sweet to the soul.—Proverbs 13:19

EFFORT IS BETTER THAN CHANCE

If chance gives you an even break, that is fair enough. Man loves chance, but chance seldom loves him. Luck sometimes grants favors, but planned concerted effort grants more.

There are many things chance won't do: won't grow a crop, won't build a house, won't operate a business, won't write a book, won't earn a college degree, won't save a dollar. Doing things worthwhile have to be done on purpose.

The winner is not willing for luck to deal his portion. As the captain of his fate, he rides the waves of fortune determined to make some luck for himself — and he does!

> *Those who trust to chance must abide by the results of chance.*
>
> —*Calvin Coolidge*

And Solomon determined to build a house...
—II Chronicles 2:1

LIFETIME OF DECISIONS

Life is a journey of decisions and the person who can't make them has a hard trip ahead. All along the pathway of life are stalled persons, stuck between *yes* and *no*.

When Alexander was asked how he conquered the world, he replied, "By not delaying."

One must have a mind before he can make it up, but indecision usually stems not from a lack of intelligence but from a lack of faith and courage and diligence. For the better life, be wise enough, confident enough, bold enough and industrious enough, to make decisions, and then be resolute enough to carry them out.

> *Who hesitate and falter life away,*
> *And lose tomorrow the ground won today.*
>
> —*Matthew Arnold*
> 1822 - 1888

How long halt ye between two opinions?
—I Kings 18:21

ASPIRE

Of the qualities that distinguish the big, the little and the mediocre, one is their aspiration. Massive accomplishments cannot come from tiny aims.

The climber must upward turn his face. Ambition invites man's steps and points him to higher places.

Goals add life to life. With no goals, man dies of nothing.

If tongues could be put in all the failures of men, they would say: "You didn't aspire. You didn't climb. You didn't continue."

So, for a blaze of success, each should pick his star, hitch to it, and then hold on.

And thou, my mind, aspire to higher things.
—Sir Philip Sidney
1554 - 1586

... I must also see Rome.—Acts 19:21

PREVAIL

Though victory is sweet, it can come only from conflict. And the rainbow which is beautiful is formed solely in a cloud.

So it is with man: The triumphant and comely emerge stronger and prettier from the conflicts and storms. They succumb not to the hideous influences which threaten them. They can prevail and they do. They can be better men and women and that they become. Like the cactus blossom, a marvel of sweetness, they rise above a prickly mass of ugliness. They become winners by exerting the greater dominance.

Each wellborn soul must win what it deserves.
—Ella Wheeler Wilcox

Be not overcome of evil, but overcome evil with good.—Romans 12:21

WRONG VIEW OF LIFE

A sailor boy slides over the side of his ship, a deserter. Why? He thought all a sailor had to do was to board his ship and sail, sail, sail, until finally he lands in a foreign port and there beneath a full moon, amidst glamour and luxury, court a native beauty in a romantic land. Instead, he ended up scrubbing decks and washing dishes. A false ideal ruined him.

And his error is society's error — a perverted notion of the ends of living. The doctrine of effortless ease — eat, drink and be merry — has left us unprepared to face the sterner requirements of life.

> *There has never yet been a man in our history who led a life of ease whose name is worth remembering.*
>
> —*Theodore Roosevelt*

> Man shall not live by bread alone...
> —Mathew 4:4

PESSIMISM NOT FOR ME

A city man visited his cousin in the country. Together they walked over the crops. After they had inspected the corn, the city cousin enthusiastically commented, "Never have I seen corn like this. Surely this must be the finest corn in the state."

The farmer pessimistically muttered, "Yes, but it is so hard on the soil." Good had sprung out of the ground, but to him it was only a sign of hidden disaster. His own outlook had denied him the happiness his success deserved.

Nothing is too good to be true, if you expect good; but there is no hope up ahead, if you expect failure.

To expect defeat is nine-tenths of defeat itself.
—Francis Marion Crawford

And we were in our sight as grasshoppers, and so we were in their sight.—Numbers 13:33

BEARING BURDENS

Actual burdens only keep your feet on the ground, but it is the over-burden complex that bends your head to the ground where it is difficult to see life's possibilities. It is hard to see a star when your head is down.

You can find courage to raise up — and, surprisingly, the burdens won't be as heavy as you think — realizing that the other fellow lives with his problems which are just as numerous and complex as yours; and if he can, you can. This will save you from self-pity which will break anybody.

> *If all the world's secret troubles were put in one pile and each person asked to take an equal share, we would surely prefer to keep those we already have.*
>
> —*Socrates*
> 469 - 399 B.C.

We are troubled on every side yet not distressed; we are perplexed, but not in despair.—II Corinthians 4:8

SORROW IS IN THE PLAN

Sorrow is a part of the world's plan; sooner or later it visits all. But not all react in the same way. Some mellow; others harden. It can beautify your life like the dew gives the flower a more beautiful hue. Grief can produce pity, add to sincerity and bring one down to the ground of reality.

Sadness must be for the good of man, or he would not have been given the capacity for it, but so is joy. Sorrow is so potent, however, that man needs it only in small amounts for brief periods, but he requires joy in big doses for long durations.

Thy fate is the common fate of all,
Into each life some rain must fall,
Some days must be dark and dreary.

—*Henry Wadsworth Longfellow*
1807 - 1882

...and the month which was turned unto them from sorrow to joy, and from mourning into a good day.—Esther 9:22

PAIN PROTECTS

Pain has been ordained for the protection and enhancement of man. Without it, he wouldn't know whether he was walking on green grass or hot coals, on sharp nails or feather pillows.

Seeing that hurts of many kinds, from many sources, are appointed to every one of us as Infinite Wisdom has thought wise, then my part is to thicken my skin for lashes, adjust my mind for injury, strengthen my back for burdens, and increase my faith for sorrow.

And each time I suffer by trial, I shall be a lot more man and a little more divine — and prepared for a little more pain.

There's a pang in all rejoicing,
and a joy in the heart of pain.

—Bayard Taylor
1825 - 1878

For we know that the whole creation groaneth and travaileth in pain together until now.—Romans 8:22.

SPEAKING AND LISTENING SKILL

Silence is not always better than speech, but it is always good enough for us to think twice before we break it.

The better thing is to be discerning enough to know when to talk and when to listen. Nothing marks a person quicker than his tongue and ears, what he says and what he doesn't say.

A good rule to follow is: If your words are not worth more than your silence, don't waste them. And in the event you should violate the first rule, then follow the second: If you talk yourself into trouble, listen yourself out.

There are two sciences which every man ought to learn: First, the silence of speech; second, the more difficult one of silence.

—*Socrates*
469 - 399 B.C.

... a time to keep silence and a time to speak.—Ecclesiastes 3:7

LOVE UNDERSTANDS

The little world each lives in needs an atmosphere of understanding. This calls for artists — not bunglers. To understand people is truly one of the most accomplished arts and one of the most necessary ingredients of successful living.

It is an art more dependent on heart feeling than eye sight and ear hearing. We cannot fathom people unless we have the love that feels for them and with them. It is then that we place the charitable construction on their motives, magnify their virtues and minimize their faults. When this is done, there is no problem in understanding people.

Love is master of all arts.
—Italian Proverb

For love shall cover the multitude of sins.
— I Peter 4:8

CONTROL YOURSELF

There is something lacking in the man who can control his dog better than himself. It makes you wonder which one is living the dog's life.

Evidently it takes more power to control self than other men or beasts. In giving an order to self, you know if you really mean it.

He who rules himself is the most masterly master. Being free, he is unshackled to handle today and unchained to face tomorrow. He is Mr. Freedom, Mr. Victory, Mr. Boss. He directs himself, and that's where success or failure begins.

The world is yours, provided you are yours.

> *Most powerful is he who has himself in his power.*
> —*Lucius Annaeus Seneca*
> 8 B.C. - 65 A.D.

> And every man that striveth for the mastery is temperate in all things.—1 Corinthians 9:25.

RIGHT — THE SAFE WAY

The right of way in living belongs to those who pursue right. No person should expect to run the barricade of wrong for long without crashing. History testifies that safety is on the side of those who follow the traffic rules of rectitude.

But not all will choose the correct way. Of course, every man has a right to his rights — though they are wrongs — unless they hurt others. But his having this privilege settles nothing, other than his claim to personal freedom. For no question is ever answered until it is answered right.

Heaven itself has ordained the right.

—George Washington
1732 - 1799

I will teach you the good and the right way.—I Samuel 12:23.

CONSCIENCE-MADE PRISONS

How unfortunate for a person to make a prison for himself out of his own conscience — a prison stronger than iron bars. For no dungeon can be as frightening and unyielding as one's locked up conscience. No jailer can be as unrelenting as one's self. No chains can be as restrictive as a mind shackled with self-condemnation.

Though you live in the land of the free, you are not liberated unless your conscience is free and clear. The freest freedom is within a man. And accordingly each who would have it must keep himself fit to live with.

Labor hard to keep alive in your breast that little spark of celestial fire called conscience.
—*George Washington*
1732 - 1799

And herein do I exercise myself, to have always a conscience void of offence toward God, and toward men.—Acts 24:16

COMBINATION FOR CALUMNY

Slanderous tongues! Slanderous ears! The combination of infamy which gives calumny to the wind. It spreads where sweet misery seeks companionship. Where dirty people seek to be cleaner. Where the defeated and frustrated wish to knock others down for their stairs.

Having no joy in goodness, this destroyer of reputations finds delight in another's destruction. With death as his trade, he would make a good hangman, if it were not for his cowardice. But this would expose him.

To noble souls, the slanderer's malignment is a dagger to their ears and a sword to their hearts. And they flee him, leaving him no friends but his own kind.

> *For slander lives upon succession,*
> *For ever housed where it gets possession.*
>
> —*William Shakespeare*
> 1564 - 1616

Whoso privily slandereth his neighbor, him will I cut off.—Psalms 101:5

NEVER BE A JUDAS

No! Not every person has his price. Some cannot be bought. Those who can, put the price tag on themselves — not on employer, not on a friend, not on a confidant — for in selling another, they sell themselves.

When we start grading lost power in human relations, we have to put disloyalty up toward the top of the list For when trust breaks down, our whole world quits turning.

If you are going to be another's friend, for heaven's sake never betray him. Be true. Give him the quiet confidence in you he needs.

> *Still, as of old,*
> *Man by himself is priced.*
> *For thirty pieces Judas sold*
> *Himself, not Christ.*
>
> *—Anonymous*

And they covenanted with him for thirty pieces of silver. And from that time he sought opportunity to betray him.—Matthew 26:15, 16

AGE HAS OPPORTUNITIES

Age presents opportunities that youth, because of inexperience, is not prepared to accept. Experience comes only with time. We would not sell intellectualism and zeal short. Neither would we undervalue experience; for it has tested numerous theories, many of which proved to be jokers for youth.

There is no substitute for gray matter, nor for gray hair. Combine the two and you have double power; add to them zeal and you have a triple threat. Youth can have the two, but not the three. Age can have them all.

An age so blest that, by its side,
Youth seems the waste instead.

—Robert Browning
1812 - 1889

But he forsook the counsel of the old men, which they had given him, and consulted with the young men that were grown up with him . . .—I Kings 12:8

BE PLEASANT

Take care that the face which looks out from your mirror in the morning is a pleasant one. You may not see it again all day, but others will — and it will attract or repel.

You may have more brains than your competitor; but if he smiles and you frown, he will find open doors where you find them closed.

A smile is a natural relaxer for the one who does it and for the one who sees it. A friend-maker. A source of health, comfort and happiness for everybody.

It was only a sunny smile,
But it scattered the night
And little it cost in the giving;
Like morning light,
And made the day worth living.

—Anonymous

Saul and Jonathan were lovely and pleasant in their lives.—II Samuel 1:23

BEAUTIFUL WORLD

There is so much beauty in the world: Majestic mountains. Sleeping valleys. Rolling plains. Winding rivers. Billowy oceans. Blue skies. Silvery moon. Twinkling stars. Green grass. Colorful flowers. Picturesque trees. Good-looking animals. Graceful fowls.

The only ugliness we have in this world is man's conduct, man's litter and man's abuse of the beautiful. But the world does have its adorable people who live becoming lives. They are the world's masterpieces of unequalled beauty, an adorableness man makes of himself; and the more he develops, the more he beholds. For much of the beauty man sees is only a mirror reflecting self.

A thing of beauty is a joy forever.

—*John Keats*
1795 - 1821

He hath made everything beautiful in his time.—Ecclesiastes 3:11

ARE WE REFLECTING SELF?

"What a frightful neighborhood," said Grandma Alarmist.

"A sorry people," commented Grandpa Faultfinder.

"So overbearing," harangued Aunt Browbeater.

"They're criminals," stated Cousin Skeleton-N-Closet.

Then Uncle Number-One remarked, "Never before saw such a selfish group."

"A dreadful bore, these dull people," protested Son Stupid.

"It's a concentration of stuck-ups," stated older Daughter Frosty.

"They're no good," spouted the parrot.

But Mrs. Sunshine had the opposite view: "Good people, considerate, kind, unselfish, and they are smart."

Oftentimes what we see is only a mirror reflecting self. The world looks better when seen through better eyes.

If we had no faults of our own, we would not take so much pleasure in noticing those of others.
> —*La Rochefoucauld*
> 1613 - 1680

Thou art the man.—II Samuel 12:7

A LITTLE SUGAR INSIDE

As a loving mother pressed her little boy to her bosom, she asked, "Johnny, what makes you so sweet and cheerful?"

Johnny replied, "I think when God made me out of dust, he must have put a little sugar in."

Johnny isn't a philosopher — or is he? — just a first-grader; nevertheless, he expressed the secret of a sweet disposition — sugar on the inside. The pleasant, cheerful temperament is only the outward manifestation of an inward state. Both the best and the worst, the sweetest and the bitterest, are in the mind. Sweeten it to your advantage, for the power of a good-humored personality is inconceivable.

You are like a flower,
So sweet and pure and fair.

—Heinrich Heine
1797 - 1856

David ... the sweet psalmist of Israel.
—II Samuel 23:1

ABHOR EVIL

One sure lesson history teaches is: The more association with evil, the less evil it appears. The commonness of vice makes it seem harmless and respectable. But neither ugliness gets pretty nor wrong right, we just get accustomed to viewing them. We change, not the evils we once decried. Thus through a gradual process, environment can tempt the purest to pursue the things once despised.

Lest we come to adore what we now abhor, may we refrain from taking the simple but deadly steps: association with evil, condonation of evil, approval of evil, embrace of evil and addiction to evil.

Vice is a monster of so frightful mien,
As to be hated needs but to be seen;
Yet seen too oft, familiar with her face,
We first endure, then pity, then embrace.

—Alexander Pope
1688 - 1744

Abhor that which is evil; cleave to that which is good.—Romans 12:9

NO GLORY SEEKING

The glory-seeker is some actor, but a poor box office attraction. In his theatrics he sings his own praises, an annoying solo. He is nothing but a strutting performer whose conceit bores his audience. He wishes to blossom, but deflowers himself. Desiring to be a giant, he makes himself a dwarf. While none of us can wear his hat, just any of us can fill his shoes.

What a wonderful person this would-be wishes us to see, and this we could see, if he would be only an as-is. For there is eminence in being your honored self, your humble, sincere, unselfish self.

Pride is a king of pleasure produced by a man thinking too well of himself.

—*Benedict Spinoza*
1632 - 1677

A man's pride shall bring him low; but honor shall uphold the humble in spirit.
—Proverbs 29:23

BE COMPASSIONATE

Compassion is a deep-hearted, big-hearted quality. It is the ability to feel with another in his needs. It identifies with the pain of someone else's misery, the wound of his sorrow, the anguish of his concern, or the wants of his poverty.

It is one thing the whole human family needs and craves — mercy. And you who fill that need will find doors that swing inward to your approach.

O friends, I pray tonight,
Keep not your kisses for my dead cold brow.
The way is lonely; let me feel them now.
Think gently of me; I am travel-worn,
My faltering feet are pierced with many a thorn.
Forgive! O hearts estranged, forgive, I plead!
When ceasless bliss is mine I shall not need
The tenderness for which I long tonight.

—Belle Eugenia Smith

Finally, be ye all of one mind, having compassion one of another; love as brethren, be pitiful, be courteous.—I Peter 3:8

SELF-ESTEEM COUNTS MOST

What do I think of me? Believe it or not, it means more than what the world thinks. The man's approval I need most is the man I see in the mirror. That is the man I work with, play with, eat with, sleep with and shall die with — what he thinks of me is most important. If he doesn't approve, then the recognition and approbation of all others mean nothing.

The greatest characters have always prized self-esteem above public opinion. Being able to look self in the eye is better than the fickle notice of onlookers.

*What I am, what I am not, in the eye of
the world, is what I never cared for much.*

—*Robert Browning*
1812 - 1889

. . . not with eyeservice, as menpleasers; but in singleness of **heart, fearing** God.
—Colossians 3:22

PUT-OFF DAYS

Procrastination is the art of putting off what you should get on. It has no future, and come to think of it — no present nor past.

Today is the golden opportunity, tomorrow the silvery chance, and the next day the brazen improbability, and the day beyond that the iron impossibility.

All such put-off days quickly turn into yesterdays while immobile men stand on feet of clay that soon turn to dust.

He who has begun has half done.
Dare to be wise; begin.

—Horace
65 - 8 B.C.

Say not ye, There are yet four months, and then cometh harvest? . . . look on the fields; for they are white already to harvest.—John 4:35

MARKINGS OF A MAN

Diogenes the Cynic (400 - 325 B.C.) is reputed to have walked the streets, carrying a lantern, as if he were searching for something. When asked what he was seeking, he replied, "A man."

He wasn't looking for immaturity in a grown body given to child's play. He sought manliness — qualities — a man strong in conviction, unyielding in purpose, brave in heart, honest to the core, dependable through and through, good from head to toe.

The world is still looking for that man in multiplied millions — and you can be one of them!

A man's a man for a' that;
For a' that and a' that.

—Robert Burns
1759 - 1796

When I became a man, I put away childish things.—I Corinthians 13:11

IMAGINARY TROUBLES

There are enough real troubles without imagining some. Many people are suffering from hurts which are only figmental, but that makes the pain no less. I shall have more energy and poise to face real adversities, if I don't tire myself with conceived ones.

Carved over a mantel in an old farm house was Mark Twain's summation of troubles: "I am an old man and have known a great many troubles, but most of them never happened." This reflection gave hope to the farmer who ever had to face the possibility of floods, droughts, storms, breakdowns and insects.

> *Some of your hurts you have cured,*
> *And the sharpest you still have survived,*
> *But what torments of grief you endured*
> *From the evil which never arrived.*

> —*Ralph Waldo Emerson*
> 1803 - 1882

O Lord, thou preservest man and beast.
—Psalms 36:6

LAUGH A LITTLE

There is a time to laugh; and when the time comes, don't miss it. Express yourself in joy. Laughter is a victory over a world of ills that plague mankind. And when you can laugh at yourself, that is some victory — you have become an adult.

Laughter is good medicine for relieving the strain of life, loosening tight nerves, and increasing strength for the performance of duties, and it is more enjoyable than the pharmaceutical kind. Another thing — it will keep you from being a bore!

Keep your face with sunshine lit,
Laugh a little bit!
Gloomy shadows oft' will flit
If you have the wit and grit
Just to laugh a little bit!

—Anonymous

To every thing there is a season, and a time to every purpose under the heaven: . . . a time to weep and a time to laugh . . .
— Ecclesiastes 3:1-4

IMMORTALITY IS REASONABLE

It adds zest to this life to hope for another life. It gives more today because we believe there shall be more tomorrow — eternal life.

If there is not another life, then why this one? Animal life and vegetable life exist for the benefit of man; and if he be lost, forever lost, all of nature fails. Animals are born and die. Vegetation springs out of the earth and returns. Now if man lives on the same level — lives and dies never to live again — then nature labors and toils to no permanent accomplishment, and the plan of the universe is a hopeless and colossal failure.

The ancient heavens will roll aside for me,
As Moses monarch'd the dividing sea.
This body is my house — it is not I.
Triumphant is this faith I live, and die.

—Frederic Lawrence Knowles

And this is the promise that he hath promised us, even eternal life.—I John 2:25

MAN'S NATURE REQUIRES IMMORTALITY

Man never would have been fashioned as he is, if it had not been meant for him to be immortal. Surely he would not have been endowed with such hopes just to have them crushed. He who was created with the ability to triumph over every obstacle, to fly with the birds, and to traverse the planets, surely was designed to take wings and triumph over death.

If man is not immortal, then he is completely inexplicable; for it wouldn't make sense for him to live like a man and die like a dog. Thus man's very nature is such that immortality is too necessary not to be true.

Dust thou art, to dust returneth,
Was not spoken of the soul.

—Henry Wadsworth Longfellow
1807 - 1882

Then shall the dust return to the earth as it was: and the spirit shall return unto God who gave it.—Ecclesiastes 12:7

MORTAL EXCHANGED FOR IMMORTALITY

Man's only hope of permanence is found in his dual nature — flesh and spirit. This enables him to lay aside the corruptible body for an incorruptible one suited to an everlasting habitation.

I have stood in the old cemetery of Christ Church, Philadelphia, at the grave of one of the world's brightest and most versatile geniuses — Benjamin Franklin. As I stood there in appreciation of him and in examination of my soul, I reflected upon the epitaph he composed for his own tomb:

> *Like the cover of an old book,*
> *Its contents torn out,*
> *And stripped of its lettering and gilding,*
> *Lies here food for worms;*
> *But the work shall not be lost,*
> *For it will (as he believes) appear once more*
> *In a new and more elegant edition,*
> *Revised and corrected by the Author.*

—Benjamin Franklin
1706 - 1790

For this corruptible must put on incorruption, and this mortal must put on immortality.
— I Corinthians 15:53

NATURE BESPEAKS THE RESURRECTION

The resurrection of man is just as reasonable as the resurrection of nature. The cold, harsh wintry winds which seem opposed to us sweep down from the frozen North, biting and chilling all nature, stripping the trees of their foliage, turning the grass into the color of death. But they later return as gentle breezes in friendly fashion from the warm Southland, resurrecting all sleeping vegetation into a more beautiful life.

Surely man, the crowning glory of creation, shall fare as well as a vegetable! Surely the Creator who has the power to resurrect nature shall not fail to use that power on man!

> *Our Lord has written the promise of resurrection, not in books alone, but in every leaf in springtime.*
> —*Martin Luther*
> 1484 - 1546

I am the resurrection, and the life: he that believeth in me, though he were dead, yet shall he live.—John 11:25

April 5

DEATH PROVIDES TRANSITION

It is especially fitting that we reflect upon the resurrection of man; for apart from his resurrection there is no abiding purpose in life and no eternal hope in death.

Man's immortal nature accentuates his transitive state. Our birth was our entrance into this world; our living here is our schooling; and our death shall be our exit from it and our entrance into another one.

So death has its kindlier aspects. It was designed as gain: to bring relief to pain, to stop the flow of tears, to shorten the days of trial, to bid the soul go free.

The lordliest of all things! —
Life lends us only feet, Death gives us wings.

—Frederic Lawrence Knowles

And it came to pass, as her soul was in departing, (for she died).—Genesis 35:18

PILGRIMS

We are sustained in the belief that we are pilgrims passing through this earth to another shore where loved ones await our arrival.

I am standing upon the seashore. A ship at my side spreads her white sails to the morning breeze and starts for the blue ocean . . . I stand and watch her until at length she hangs like a speck of white cloud come down to mingle with each other. Then someone at my side says, "There! She's gone!"

Gone where? Gone from my sight . . . that is all. She is just as large in mast and hull and spar as she was when she left my side . . . Her diminished size is in me, not in her. And just at the moment when someone at my side says, "There! She's gone! — there are other eyes watching her coming, and other voices ready to take up the glad shout, "There she comes!"
And that is dying.

—Anonymous

Man goeth to his long home, and the mourners go about the streets.—Ecclesiastes 12:5

SHIELD OF PRAYER

If "In God we trust," then we trust in prayer. Prayer gives strength in weakness, courage in despair. It is the shield which protects from the blows and darts of an inconsiderate world. It is the bed upon which frailty sleeps in peace, and where worry has forgotten to vex.

So when you feel weak, drop to your knees — in prayer. There your burdens will not press you to stumble; there your tired soul can rest; there you can reverently address your needs to a Greater Power. Of course, for your words to get through, you should not live too far away.

I have been driven many times to my knees by the overwhelming conviction that I had nowhere else to go. My own wisdom and that of all about me seemed insufficient for the day.

—*Abraham Lincoln*
1809 - 1865

And when he had sent the multitude away he went up into a mountain apart to pray: and when the evening was come, he was there alone.—Matthew 14:23.

YOU AND YOUR BIBLE

Do not read anything into the Good Book, if you wish to get anything out of it — just take it straight. Instead of trying to alter your Bible to fit you, change yourself to fit it; otherwise you will have religion's conformity in reverse.

What you think of the Bible does not affect it — just you. If it appears too deep, you surely need the exercise it affords to think deeper. If it looks too exacting, you definitely require its influence to keep from straying. And if it seems dry, it might be that you have allowed too much dust to accumulate on it.

I am profitably engaged in reading the Bible. Take all of this book upon reason that you can and the balance upon faith, and you will live and die a better man.

—Abraham Lincoln
1809 - 1865

Ye shall not add unto the word which I command you, neither shall ye diminish aught from it.—Deuteronomy 4:2

RELIGION IS BETTER IN BIG DOSES

Religion to some people is like a man with a headache. He does not want to get rid of his head, but oh! how it hurts him to keep it! They have enough faith to make them miserable, but not enough to make them happy. The chief danger to religion is man's wanting it in such small amounts.

Man enjoys what he works at, and in religion there is no joy apart from a working faith. By putting his heart into it and working at the job, he finds the indispensable support of ideals, sense of purpose, peace, approval, hope and joy.

The religion of some people is constrained: they are like people who use the cold bath... they go in with reluctance, and are glad when they get out.
—*John Newton*
1725 - 1807

If any man among you seem to be religious . . . but deceiveth his own heart, this man's religion is vain.—James 1:26

BEAUTY DEEPER THAN SKIN

Why care I for the beautiful brown shell of the nut, if it is worm-eaten? About the only purpose it serves is to emphasize a difference between superficiality and reality, outward beauty and inward beauty.

Sooner or later your own appetite will settle for nothing less than the real meat of goodness, for the world can't live on empty shells and barren husks.

Physical beauty is only the framework, walls, paint and adornments, which nature displays outside the house, but what about the host or hostess who dwells within? What does he or she look like?

Beauty's but skin deep.

—John Davies of Hereford
1565 - 1618

And she was a woman of good understanding and of a beautiful countenance.—I Samuel 25:3

BIGGER THAN SELF

Life has its greatest charm when one gives himself to some person or cause he values above self. Only in the pursuit of such love and conviction can he find peace and satisfaction. It increases his grip on life and impels him to more vigorous living, without which the days are dull and boring.

The animal lives on the level where survival is the major consideration, but to the highest type of man there are other matters more important.

Some find the bigger values in such areas as religion, love for others, loyalty to country and a good name. For these they are willing to die rather than compromise.

He thought it happier to be dead,
To die for beauty than live for bread.

—*Ralph Waldo Emerson*
1803 - 1882

Neither count I my life dear unto myself.
— Acts 20:24

WHEN THERE ARE TEARS

Tears are a universal language. They often tell what words will not express. Sincerely shed, they are not willing water from a handy hydrant to be turned on and off at will, but rather the natural droplets from a heart too full to be contained. Tears are the language of the heart, and where there is a heart, there can be a tear.

Watery eyes have been known to see what clear eyes could not detect. When your plight seems so hopeless that you can't see your way through, take another look—through your tears. They may prove to be telescopic.

> *If you have tears, prepare to shed them now.*
> —*William Shakespeare*
> 1564 - 1616

> They that sow in tears shall reap in joy.—Psalms 126:5

PURPOSES INSTEAD OF WISHES

What are your purposes or plans for life? To be a piece of driftwood or a towering oak? Drifters float on chance, and the stream gets more perilous by the moment.

Put purpose in your life. Be resolute. Never submit to passiveness. Drifting is dangerous. For the course of least resistance points downstream.

It takes a strong purpose and a strong muscle to make it upstream. The only way is to lift the anchor and grab an oar, and still better — two oars. You will make your share of mistakes, but you won't make the one of doing nothing.

> *Great minds have purposes, others have wishes.*
> —*Washington Irving*
> 1783 - 1859

Every man according as he purposeth in his heart, so let him . . . —II Corinthians 9:7

April 14

DO YOUR BEST AND WORRY NOT

Be concerned, but not worried. Be warm enough to have interest, but cool enough to be calm.

Fretting never solves problems — it creates more. Worry puts fuzziness in your head, a knot in your stomach and a pack on your back. Nothing is as hurtful as worry; nothing as helpful as concern. Indifference never sees the problems; worry tangles them; but concern unravels them.

So, be enterprising enough to do your best and trustful enough to leave it with God. Do all you can and then do a little more by not worrying. Mortal man can do no more that this.

That man is blest
Who does his best
And leaves the rest;
Then do not worry.

—*Charles F. Deems*

She hath done what she could.—Mark 14:8

MORE USEFUL AWAKE

Wake up! The good life comes to him who is awake enough to see and hear and move.

No person has ever yawned his way to greatness. The sleeper sleeps through his opportunities. And while he slumbers, his talents sleep with him. And while asleep, he remains down.

Sometimes the moon appears sleepy, but it is prettier and more useful when wide awake — and so am I. So, stay awake, old friend, if I can call myself a friend to me, and I am as long as I'm awake.

To be awake is to be alive.

—Henry David Thoreau
1817 - 1862

Awake thou that sleepest, and arise from the dead.—Ephesians 5:14

TODAY BELONGS TO THE FREE

Who can call today his own? Only the free. But not every one is free the law says is free. Regardless of the statute books, the only free person is he whose heart is unfettered. Unshackled within, he has the freest freedom without. He is not hindered by hate, fettered by fear, curbed by conscience, or daunted by doubt. Today is his, because he is his. To him the fast-breaking day comes unrestrained because he has the freedom to receive it.

Thus, it is not the tick of the clock that gives me today — it is the tick of the heart.

> *Happy the man, and happy he alone,*
> *Who can call today his own;*
> *He who, secure within, can say,*
> *"Tomorrow, do thy worst, for I have lived today."*
>
> —*John Dryden*
> 1631 - 1700

See, I have set before thee this day life and good, and death and evil.—Deuteronomy 30:15

GET UNDERSTANDING

It is dangerous to drive in a fog, especially if it's mental. Be aware of what's going on around you. When you don't understand, search deeper, look longer, consult others, think, analyze, reach logical conclusions. Clarity makes the wise wiser and the safe safer.

Being misunderstood is not half as bad as not understanding. What we need most, perhaps, is comprehension. No one is prepared to make intelligent decisions about matters he doesn't understand. No person can do better than he knows. Only as a man begins to understand can he figure out things. Without knowledge his decisions are only blind guesses.

What can we reason but from what we know?

—*Alexander Pope*
1688 - 1744

Discretion shall preserve thee, understanding shall keep thee.—Proverbs 2:11

ATTAINMENT THROUGH TEMPTATION

Human beings are equated to weakness — some more than others, but there is a frailty in all. This implies that each must ever be on the guard against temptation, which when faced and overcome makes him stronger; but when not resisted, makes him that much weaker.

Hence, every temptation presents an opportunity to acquire strength and virtue — if you prevail. If there were no temptations in the world, there could be no attainment through testing and there could be no valid claim to virtue. Beyond question, he who struggles and wins proves himself a conqueror.

As the Sandwich-Islander believes that the strength and valor of the enemy he kills passes into himself, so we gain the strength of the temptation we resist.

—Ralph Waldo Emerson
1803 - 1882

Blessed is the man that endureth temptation; for when he is tried, he shall receive the crown of life, which the Lord hath promised to them that love him.—James 1:12

TIME CHANGES THINGS

Only time can solve some troubles. Whatever you offer as today's solution is resisted. But tomorrow it shall be different. As time changes the calendar, it changes circumstances. Time is an ointment for bleeding hearts, an arbitrator for dissolved friendships, a restorer of broken health and a regainer of lost fortune. Time has the power to dry tears, steady nerves, renew courage, lift eyes.

Time sees to it that the winter passes and spring bursts anew.

What a powerful and hopeful sermon the calendar preaches! And as long as it keeps turning for you, there is hope.

O time, thou must untangle this, not I;
It is too hard a knot for me to untie!

—William Shakespeare
1564 - 1616

Lord, let it alone this year also, till
I shall dig about it . . . —Luke 13:8

THE CHEERFUL

You can attract more people with cheerfulness than with gloom.

Most people feel the end will come soon enough without having doomsday peddlers to fit them in wordy shrouds before their time.

We prefer the people who light up rooms when they walk in. How eagerly we gather around them. Such is the wondrous and magnetic power of jollity. The gay person is a welcome ray of gladness to this shadow-cast and troubled world. Needy humanity craves the presence of the person who lightens burdens, mitigates misfortunes, scatters clouds, and looks to the dawn when the night is the darkest.

> *Cheerfulness keeps up a kind of daylight in the mind, and fills it with a steady and perpetual serenity.*
>
> —*Joseph Addison*
> 1672 - 1719

This is the day which the Lord hath made; we will rejoice and be glad.—Psalms 118:24

BE WHAT YOU ARE

The world is a stage where each is cast to play his own role, and the plaudits and encores are for only the ones who do. Sooner or later it is curtains for the imitators. The audience can't be fooled long. They are quick to spot a phony. When he opens his mouth he sounds like a play actor. He's unreal.

In the drama of life, theatrics are out of order. The stage is actual: the audience is genuine; and play actors are not tolerated. So be yourself. But be such a self you feel no need to act another.

> *Be not imitator; freshly act thy part;*
> *Through this world be thou an independent ranger;*
> *Better is the faith that springeth from thy heart*
> *Than a better faith belonging to a stranger.*
>
> —*From the Persian*

And God said unto Moses, I AM THAT I AM.—Exodus 3:14.

BE A GOOD LISTENER

The great majority value listening, especially if you are doing it. Just listening to a person is enough for him to regard you as a friend. With dull, cold ears it is impossible to warm the heart of another. A hearing ear makes more friends than a wagging tongue.

Some places you go you have to pay to listen; but the everyday run of people will pay you to listen to them: pay you in appreciation, popularity, kindness, and some even in wisdom. You can make a swap: give them your ears, and they will give you their hearts, their praises, their purses and additionally, some knowledge.

A good listener is not only popular everywhere, but after a while he knows something.

—Wilson Mizner

Let every man be swift to hear, slow to speak, slow to wrath.—James 1:19

AGE CAN BUD AGAIN

It takes years to grow an oak — and a man. Both lumber and brains season with time.

Deep rivers have had the flow of many waters, and deep minds have had the passing of many thoughts.

Most of the great men of history distinguished themselves after fifty. Distinction requires more than impulsive action — guided movement; more than high speed — direction.

The University of Hard Knocks has its lessons; they are hard, but effective. The price of getting wiser is getting older — plus getting a few bumps and bruises. Years should teach, and — if one is an apt student — they will.

And now in age I bud again.

—*George Herbert*
1593 - 1633

I said, Days should speak, and multitude of years should teach wisdom.—Job 32:7

FAMILY TREE AND ME

A man can't make a place for himself in the sun, if he takes refuge in the shade of the family tree.

No doubt the tree has had some distinctive limbs — we won't say anything about the shoddy ones — but what I need to do is to decide to be the best branch on it and start growing toward the sun. I shouldn't make a camp ground of where some dead limbs fell.

Today makes no demands of my forefathers; it rather asks: what are you doing? They lived their lives — now it is my turn.

I don't know who my grandfather was; I am much more concerned to know what his grandson will be.
—*Abraham Lincoln*
1809 - 1865

But avoid foolish questions, and genealogies, and contentions, and strivings about the law; for they are unprofitable and vain.
—Titus 3:9

LIFTED BY DIFFICULTIES

A touch of difficulty gives a little muscle to life — provided you have the backbone to meet it. Humility is encouraged. Self-reliance is taught. Patience is required. Inventiveness is urged. Many unknown and hidden powers buried deep in the soul are called up. And when the trouble is whipped, that day belongs to the conqueror.

Paul, the apostle, had a thorn in the flesh, and so does everybody else; the difference being in the kind, the size and the sharpness. But whatever your particular thorn is, it can be your hidden blessing.

Luckiest is he who has just enough obstacles.

Many men owe the grandeur of their lives to their tremendous difficulties.

—*Charles Haddon Spurgeon*
1834 - 1892

But he knoweth the way that I take: when he hath tried me, I shall come forth as gold.—Job 23:10

IF SOCIETY SHOULD SWAP SHOES

There are some who limp, but very few out of choice. The majority have cause.

Before you criticize the limper, try his shoes. It might give you an education no university can provide and a feeling no sermon can effect.

The faultfinder would be more tolerant of another's limp, if he had to wear for a little while those nail-piercing shoes the other fellow has to wear all time. What a change in tone and pace, if society were to swap shoes. Faces which now grin would have their tears.

> *Happy the man who could search out the cause of things.*
> *—Virgil*
> 70 - 19 B.C.

What have I now done? Is there not a cause?—I Samuel 17:29

OVERCOMING LONELINESS

At times all of us are lonely. It brings an emptiness within. A feeling of inadequacy and a lack of direction overwhelm us. We should not, however, allow loneliness to cheat us out of a single day. And here are some ways to overcome it:

— Like yourself enough that you can be happy alone.
— As a pilgrim, know your map.
— Have something to do and do it.
— Make good books interesting companions.
— Pull down any selfish walls you may have built around yourself.
— Make your presence desired, and the best way to do this is to find emptier hearts and fill them with love.

> *Seldom can the heart be lonely,*
> *If it seeks a lonelier still;*
> *Self-forgetting, seeking only*
> *Emptier cups of love to fill.*
>
> —*Frances R. Havergal*

And I, even I only, am left.—I Kings 19:10

VINDICTIVENESS? NEVER!

The slander others say about us is not as damaging as any evil we might vindictively say about them. Speaking evil of another hurts the defamer more than the defamed. There is always a certain amount of sympathy for the attacked — innocent or guilty — but for the attacker, never!

If we maintain clean hands and a pure heart, the other fellow's mud is not going to hurt us very much. But what about him? Not only will the world see his soiled hands, but it will sooner or later decide that it heard little more than a croaking frog in the mud.

Don't soil your hands by slinging mud.

—Anonymous

And Saul lifted up his voice, and wept. And he said to David, Thou art more righteous than I: for thou hast rewarded me good, whereas I have rewarded thee evil.
—I Samuel 24:16, 17

ENVY IS HURTFUL

Envy is fresh heat from torment. It blisters itself with its own perverted thermology; it makes itself miserable with its own miseries; it sorrows because it cannot rejoice in another's fortune.

Envy is negative and destructive. Discontent because of what others have will not add to your possessions. There is, however, greatness in climbing on your own virtues — not in seeing others depressed to your level.

Be stirred with love — not envy. Be too big to begrudge, too good to be dissatisfied with your neighbor's prosperity.

Furthermore, appearances are too deceptive for us to envy anybody.

> *If every man's internal care*
> *Were written on his brow,*
> *How many would our pity share*
> *Who raise our envy now?*
>
> —*Pietro Metastasio*

Again, I considerd all travail, and every right work, that for this man is envied of his neighbor. This is also vanity and vexation of spirit.—Ecclesiastes 4:4

KNOCKERS LOSE

Forbear to find fault, for we all have them. It is a game two can play and he may come up with the highest score, find more in you than you find in him.

If you knock the other fellow, his door won't open to you; neither will his neighbor's. Those doors swing on hinges of toleration.

The world will be more responsive if you have a good word for everybody, for those above you and for those below you. The ones above you deserve it, and the ones below you — well, even the tombstones praise those beneath them.

A critic is a legless man who teaches running.

—*Channing Pollock*

They found fault.—Mark 7:2

QUEST

We often hear there is a pot of gold at the end of the rainbow. What we rarely hear is how few find it. Furthermore, we seldom hear the conditions for finding it: that man must traverse the distance to it and then dig, and in most cases, again and again. The rainbow is yours for the seeing, but the gold — now that is different — is yours only through quest.

It is a joy to gaze at the rainbow, but if you want the gold at its base start searching — and don't forget to carry the pick. The best in life is for only the seekers!

There are deep things of God,
Push out from shore;
Hast thou found much?
Give thanks, and look for more.

—Charles Gordon Ames

The land, which we passed through to search it, is an exceeding good land.—Numbers 14:7

ACTION

Success requires action. The way to better yourself is to get started. A moving object has more force than a stationary one. When a man rises from a sitting position, he doubles the force of his pressure on the ground. While standing still, his pressure is minimum, because it is downward; but on moving, he exerts a side force greater than his weight.

This illustrates man's force in other areas. In sitting (idleness), his power is very little. In arising (making a beginning), he doubles his force. In moving (doing something), he multiplies his force many times.

The superior man is modest in his speech, but exceeds in his actions.

—Confucius
551 - 479 B.C.

And the man Jeroboam was a mighty man of valor: and Solomon seeing the young man that he was industrious, he made him ruler over all the charge of the house of Joseph.—I Kings 11:28

NOW IS THE TIME

A farmer in Tennessee lay desperately ill in a hospital. For weeks he struggled between life and death, much of the time in a coma. One morning he regained consciousness and asked his nurse what time it was. She replied, "It is springtime, and nature is bursting forth with renewed vigor."

"Springtime," said the patient. "Then I can't die now, for it is time to plow."

For all of us, *now* is plowing time. The only time to which we are joined is *now*. With this attitude, today can be mine; and so can tomorrow when it becomes today.

Now or never was the time.
—*Laurence Sterne*
1713 - 1768

And now, Lord, what wait I for?—Psalms 39:7

STRAIGHT AHEAD

When I was a boy, we occasionally traveled the country roads into town. Dogs would run out and bark at us, but my father said that if we stopped to chase them off, we never would get to town. Reaching our destination was more important than chasing dogs.

When you have a goal to reach, pursue it. When you have a work to do, do it. Be not deterred by criticism nor any other diversion.

It takes the will to continue to get there. There is no magic that will turn the trick. It is all a matter of concentration and grit.

I go through my appointed daily stage, and I care not for the curs who bark at me along the road.
—*Frederick the Great*
1712 - 1786

Turn not to the right hand nor to the left.—Proverbs 4:27

SPEAK AND LET SPEAK

Time about is fair play, even when it comes to speaking and listening. We can't expect others to listen to us if we are unwilling to listen to them.

It is difficult to listen to what we don't believe, but maybe the other fellow has the same problem when he listens to us.

Speak and let speak grants freedom of speech to all. It takes bigness on the inside to give a person a respectful hearing when he expresses views contrary to ours. Naturally, every one likes to hear the *smart* people who agree with him, but this is no test of magnanimity at all.

> *I do not agree with a word you say, but I will defend to the death your right to say it.*
>
> —*Francois Marie Aroult Voltaire*
> 1694 - 1778

> And some said, What will this babbler say? ... And they took him, and brought him unto Areopagus, saying, May we know what this new doctrine, whereof thou speakest, is?—Acts 17:18, 19

WHAT IS HOME?

Home? What is it? It is the word that strikes melody in the heart. It is something we associate with mother. It is the place of rest to which the care-worn soul turns tired steps from the toils and struggles of life. It is the family fortress that shuts out the world. It is where the weak and weary spirit finds strength. It is the one place in this wide world where hearts are sure of each other. It is the only place where the commoner can be a king or a queen or a prince or a princess.

We call it *Home, Sweet Home.*

What is home without a mother?
            —Alice Hawthorne

She looketh well to the ways of her household.—Proverbs 31:27

HOME IS WHERE MOTHER IS

A child was asked, "Where is your home?" The little fellow replied, "Where mother is." Ah, this is home!

She has been endowed with special feminine and solicitous traits which nobly qualify her for the strenuous and honorable task of being a homemaker. What night-watching! what self-denial! what tears! what concern! what joy! what helpfulness is seen in the home mother makes! She forges the ties of an undying love and welds the bonds of a family trust as she makes them proud in their poverty, sincere in their simplicity and one in their plurality.

This is home. And this is bliss.

> *There are three words that sweetly blend,*
> *And on the heart are graven.*
> *A precious, soothing balm they lend,*
> *They're 'Mother,' 'Home,' and 'Heaven.'*
>
> *—Anonymous*

To be discreet, chaste, keepers at home . . .
— Titus 2:5

May 8

WOMAN'S GREATEST ROLE

The greatest mission of woman is motherhood. In this eminent calling she glorifies the Creator and perpetuates His creation.

It is a task that involves a thousand sacrifices, but womanhood with a song on the lips and a prayer in the heart rises triumphantly. At travail of body and anxiety of mind, she makes human life possible. And then, little by little, she gives her life to see this new life blossom into noble maturity.

As she shapes the character of her children, woman shapes the destiny of nations. Upon her role all future progress depends.

Who fed me from her gentle breast
And hushed me in her arms to rest,
And on my cheek sweet kisses prest?
My mother.

—Jane Taylor
1783 - 1824

And Adam called his wife's name Eve; because she was the mother of all living.
— Genesis 3:20

MOTHER'S WORK

A mother works and works and works. And the willingness with which she does it is the chief contribution to a pleasant and happy family.

It has been said that the thrush goes to work at half-past two every morning during the summer and works until nine-thirty at night — a straight nineteen hours — during which it feeds its young over two hundred times.

The blackbird works seventeen hours and feeds its little ones a hundred times a day.

In the home the energetic mother is up early and retires late. Like the hard-working bird, she does it for those who are so precious to her.

> *A man's work is from sun to sun,*
> *But a mother's work is never done.*
>
> *—Anonymous*

She riseth also while it is yet night, and giveth meat to her houschold, and a portion to her maidens.—**Proverbs 31:15**

MOTHER'S ROCKING CHAIR

Let me tell you about an old chair that symbolizes greatness in child training. It was mother's rocking chair. It had to have rockers because she had so many cares and troubles to soothe.

There the children sobbed out their hurts and worries. There advice was given. There character was developed. There nobler aspirations were born. There sympathy was extended. There assurance held sway. There sleep was more inviting than in bed.

It was a combination nursery, pulpit, classroom, lecture hall, library and study room. Whatever it was, we desperately need it today, squeak and all, for even the squeak was music — music to the heart.

Earth's finest school—mother was instructor there!
Oh! the learning that came from her old rocking chair!

—Anonymous

Forsake not the law of thy mother.
—Proverbs 6:20

MOTHER-MADE

To a large extent we are mother-made. She instills a way of life in the little heart. She throws a spell around the child which is hard to break. Years later the child is apt to mirror the mother.

At a great meeting of prominent women, one was introduced as a "self-made woman." Instead of enjoying the tribute, she seemed to be bothered by it. For a few moments, she appeared to be in a deep study. Then she broke the silence by saying, "No, I am not a 'self-made woman.' I think my mother had much to do with it."

And right she was!

Thou art thy mother's glass, and she in thee
Calls back the lovely April of her prime.

—*William Shakespeare*
1564 - 1616

As is the mother, so is her daughter.
— Ezekiel 16:44

HER CHILDREN PRAISE HER

Of all the human names held sacred in man's memory, none equals the sweet and sublime name of mother. How precious in after years are the recollections of a mother's patient training. How many have nobly ascribed all recognized success to the devotion and guidance of mother. Through helpless infancy her throbbing heart was our strong support and safe protection.

It is not strange, therefore, that we feel animated to struggle more manfully in life's great battle when we recall mother's prayers in childhood's early dawn and think upon her counsels in youth's slippery path. Those lofty precepts! Impressions as durable as time!

All that I am or hope to be, I owe to my angel mother.
> —*Abraham Lincoln*
> 1809 - 1865

Her children arise up, and call her blessed.—Proverbs 31:28

LOVE MAKES THE DIFFERENCE

Love turns on the sun and exclaims, "All is well with the world!"

Only love brings out man's full size. It discovers within him ambitions unnumbered and goodness unlimited. It multiplies an energy way beyond his imagination and keeps him going long after others drop. It excites a courage braver than any soldier and stands him up to face bombs and bullets, scandal and shame.

It comforts like warm sunshine, refreshes like gentle rain.

Love's fires glow the longest; its arrows are the sharpest; its kisses are the sweetest; its hours are the shortest.

It speaks and hears a language known only to lovers.

Let the night-winds touch thy brow
With the heat of my burning sigh,
And melt thee to hear the vow
Of a love that shall not die
Till the sun grows cold,
And the stars are old,
And the leaves of the Judgment Book unfold!

—Bayard Taylor
1825 - 1878

His banner over me was love.—Song of Solomon 2:4

CONSCIENCE AFFECTS BRAVERY

An unafraid conscience is a great contributor to courage. Bravery for life's struggles requires scrupulous living. A condemning self is tuned to every fright, for it thinks others know. But with no skeletons hanging in a man's heart, he feels no need to run. Knowing that he has nothing to hide, he can eyeball every man.

For a stronger, braver and more fearless life, live on the approving side of conscience. Be confident your cause is just; be certain you believe in what you do; be sure you treat the other fellow right; and therein you shall find courage to stand.

Thus conscience does make cowards of us all.

—William Shakespeare
1564 - 1616

The wicked flee when no man pursueth; but the righteous are bold as a lion.
—Proverbs 28:1

PLAY THE MAN

Our times demand men. For the great society cannot sprout from weaklings. Nor a well managed world from ill managed lives. We need men who can stand up to the world, remake it, reshape it.

The man is the *can*, the *will*, the *does*, the *won't*. He can stand, he will stand, he does stand, he won't back off.

But the weakling doesn't have the mettle for the clash. He is bent and broken when the world hits him. He doesn't have the strength to meet the pressures with a strong force. He loses. And his loss is the world's loss.

> *God give us men! A time like this demands*
> *Strong minds, great hearts, true faith, and*
> *ready hands:*
> *Men who have honor.*
>
> —*Josiah Gilbert Holland*
> 1819 - 1881

Be of good courage, and let us play the men for our people.—II Samuel 10:12

DON'T TROUBLE TROUBLE

A good way to stay out of trouble is not to trouble trouble until trouble troubles you. Don't ask for it.

Man is of few days and full of trouble, but his troubles will be fewer and his days happier if he minds his own business. If he keeps quiet, there is a good chance trouble will pass him by.

The troublemaker is usually in trouble because he has a genius for getting into it. But the peacemaker is ordinarily at peace because he has a talent for proceeding softly where conflict may break loose. He knows it is good to let a sleeping dog lie.

Nothing can bring you peace but yourself.

—*Ralph Waldo Emerson*
1803 - 1882

He that passeth by, and meddleth with strife belonging not to him, is like one that taketh a dog by the ears.—Proverbs 26:17

NOT SWAYED BY AGE PRATTLERS

Today is mine provided I am neither too young nor too old in my thinking to appropriate it. If my outlook is not prepared for today, then today is not mine — except to breathe, and that's not enough to make it mine. To capitalize today, I must not listen to those who prattle age in my ears.

When I was seventeen I heard
From each censorious tongue,
"I'd not do that if I were you;
You see you're rather young."

Now that I number forty years,
I'm quite as often told
Of this or that I shouldn't do
Because I'm quite too old.

O carping world! If there's an age
Where youth and manhood keep
An equal poise, alas! I must
Have passed it in my sleep.

—Walter Learned

And Saul said to David, Thou art not able to go against this Philistine to fight with him: for thou art but a youth, and he a man of war from his youth.—I Samuel 17:33

RIGHT FOR RIGHT'S SAKE

It takes all kinds to make a world, but there are enough other people — without you — to contribute the wrongs. And the darker they make the world, the brighter you can shine.

Do right for the sake of right, for there is reward enough in the virtue of doing it.

In the struggle between good and bad, look not at how the world is lining up, but rather at how right and wrong are shaping up. Let that determine your course. And then so follow it that you can say each night, "I am so glad this day I have done the right."

> *They are slaves who dare not be*
> *In the right with two or three.*
>
> *—James Russell Lowell*
> 1819 - 1891

And he did that which was right in the sight of the Lord.—II Kings 14:3

NONSENSICAL PRETENSE

Pretense doesn't make sense. It's make-believe, play-acting, fakery, humbuggery. If the world is real — and it is — then there is no place for sham.

Hypocrisy may look good, but it's only a wolf in sheep's clothing; sounds good, but it never intends to keep its promises; appears good, but it's merely trying to cash in on goodness. It's bad! bad because it's a sham! A fraud that solely thinks of self!

Hypocrisy makes one only a performer. The word without the heart is still unspoken — just feigned. The deed without the doer still remains undone — just acted.

You may charge me with murder —
or want of sense —
(We are all of us weak at times):
But the slightest approach to a false pretence
Was never among my crimes!

—Lewis Carroll
1832 - 1898

For the vile person will speak villainy, and his heart will work iniquity, to practice hypocrisy.—Isaiah 32:6

THE FAULTFINDER

No statue has ever been set up to a faultfinder. Our two main objections to him is he has eyes and ears which see and hear our faults bigger than they are, and then puts a tongue in this sin of his.

There is a difference in fact-finding and faultfinding. The fact-finder sees good just as freely as evil. But the faultfinder is biased in favor of the faults.

Humanity is imperfect. But in most people there is much more good than bad. Take a white sheet of paper and make a blotch in the center of it. What do you see? A spot. But think how much more whiteness there is around it.

Man judges from a partial view
None ever yet his brother knew.

—*John Greenleaf Whittier*
1807 - 1892

But with me it is a very small thing that I should be judged of you, or of man's judgment; yea, I judge not mine own self.—
I Corinthians 4:3

DEALING WITH OTHERS' FAULTS

If circumstances suggest you mention to another his faults, put yourself in his place before you start. Consider your own imperfections.

Remember—the offender's heart is fragile, handle it with care.

Be not a hindrance but a help. Do it not for vengeance, but for virtue. Hasten to heal, don't rush to retort. Be firm but fair, pointed but patient, censorious but considerate. Be gentle. Be kind.

And if your message should be rejected, at least your manners will have to be admired. And the assurance that you have done right, in the right way, will give you a softer pillow for sweeter sleep.

Deal with the faults of others as gently as with your own.

—*Confucius*
551 - 479 B.C.

But the wisdom that is from above is first pure, then peaceable, gentle, and easy to be entreated, full of mercy and good fruits, without partiality, and without hypocrisy.
—James 3:17

ACCEPT DISSAPPOINTMENT
PHILOSOPHICALLY

The point of disappointment is to learn not a bitter but better way.

You can tell the size of a person by how much it takes to stop him. By climbing over the rubbish of disappointment, he proves himself bigger than the obstacle.

Accept disappointments hopefully. For some are inevitable. There always have been some clouds without moisture, some rivers without water, and some expectations without realization. But never quit! Never turn sour! There is cause for hope. Just as the sun goes down every night, it also rises every morning. So reshuffle your plans and keep on striving.

Disappointment is often the salt of life.
—Theodore Parker
1810 - 1860

Ye looked for much, and lo, it came to little.—Haggai 1:9

DO GOOD AND YOU SHALL RECEIVE

We — like the bee that seeks honey or the vulture that seeks carion — find what we seek; and what we seek finds us. Whatever man draws near to meets him, and whatever he flees from flees from him. Double action! This is why so much good comes to some people. The returns. The dividends on the investment.

Doing good sooner or later returns to its source. Full measure and running over. So instead of thinking so much about receiving good, it is better to get busy and do good and let the receiving take care of itself.

Goodness is the only investment that never fails.
— *Henry David Thoreau*
1817 - 1862

He that followeth after righteousness and mercy findeth life, righteousness and honor.
—Proverbs 21:21

AT THE WHEEL OF LIFE

Every person sits at the wheel of his own life with one foot on the accelerator, leaving the other for the brake. He needs to be awake. He needs to be alert. There are many wrecks along the way. Each travels at his own risk.

The journey demands that you follow the directions, observe the regulations, drive carefully, for it is your life you are running.

If you lose control for a moment, you crash. Though you have steered yourself well ten-thousand times, there is never a time for intemperate driving. If you lose control, you crash.

> *For a man to conquer himself is the first and noblest of all victories.*
>
> *—Plato*
> 428 - 348 B.C.

> And the driving is like the driving of Jehu the son of Nimshi; for he driveth furiously.—II Kings 9:20

APPEARANCES CAN DECEIVE

Appearances can be very deceiving. Green grass may cover the ground where dead men's bones lie. A healthy-looking tree may be ready to fall, a victim of its own rottenness within.

Sweet manners may be only skin deep; and if you should prick the skin, you would be spurted with bitterness. A broad face does not necessarily mean a broad mind. A clean body cannot be equated with a clean life. A praying mouth does not always signify a praying heart.

It is not the cloth that makes the minister. Clothes change only the looks — not the person.

I pray thee, O God, that I may be beautiful within.

—*Socrates*
469 - 499 B.C.

For ye are like unto whited sepulchres, which indeed appear beautiful outward; but are within full of dead men's bones, and of all uncleanness.—Matthew 23:27

ABIDE YOUR TIME

Keep your patience! For if you lose it, you lose you: your composure, confidence, assurance, will and success.

Patience is victorious: oftentimes outruns skill and outwits impulsiveness.

Patience is productive: in time the mulberry leaf becomes silk.

Patience is visionary: visualizes the ripened grain as the fruition of a series of successive steps of working and waiting — securing the land, breaking the soil and planting the seed. Nature is wise enough to wait and persistent enough to eventually have her way; and so can man, if he will add patience to diligence.

Patience is a possessor: the world belongs to him who bides his time.

And he shall reign a goodly king
And sway his hand o'er every clime
With peace writ on his signet ring,
Who bides his time.

—James Whitcomb Riley

For ye have need of patience...
—Hebrews 10:36

SUPERSTITION

Personal freedom is lost when men become cringing slaves to superstition. They, controlled by irrational thinking, become the bowing sacrificers to a supposed supernatural that is not supernatural.

The superstitious can't conquer the world, because they've been conquered by some stray cat, standing ladder or broken mirror. They are trying to solve life's problems through a hocus-pocus that pulls rabbits out of hats. That won't help them, but they can help themselves. How? By each one's being his own man, having his own mind, standing on his own feet, and pursuing his own dreams as he lives his own fearless life.

We are tattooed in our cradles with the beliefs of our tribe.

—*Oliver Wendell Holmes*
1809 - 1894

Then Paul stood in the midst of Mars hill, and said, Ye men of Athens, I perceive that in all things ye are too superstitious.
—Acts 17:22

VARIETY SPICES LIFE

It takes a little variety to season life. Sameness makes for lackluster. The same old six and seven are not satisfying. Why not try to count up to eight or nine? Bread is the staff of life, but we need a little cake once in a while.

Variety gives life renewed enchantment. What about some newfangled clothes, different entertainment, varied topics for discussion, unvisited places to go, new scenes to see? Getting out of the rut is like crawling out of the grave.

Nature with a thousand variations says to man, "The world is too varied for you to ever be bored. Enjoy me."

> *Variety is the mother of enjoyment.*
> —*Benjamin Disraeli*
> 1804 - 1881

For, lo, the winter is past, the rain is over and gone; the flowers appear on the earth; the time of the singing of birds is come, and the voice of the turtle is heard in our land; the fig tree putteth forth her green figs, and the vines with the tender grape give a good smell.—Song of Solomon 2:11-13

CONFIDENCE GIVES POWER

There are all kinds of "isms" in the world, and two that greatly affect you are of your own making: optimism or pessimism. Our victory or defeat lies mostly in the mind, in what we think we can or cannot do. Successful people are positive thinkers; failures think in negative terms.

There is no human power like that of confidence. The optimist says, "I'm sure there is a way," and rightly so; for the years have taught him that things have a way of working out, though sometimes slowly. And as they evolve, he who faces the sun won't see the shadows.

Confidence imparts a wonderful inspiration to its possessor.
—*John Milton*
1608 - 1674

If God be for us, who can be against us?
—Romans 8:31

IMMORTALITY

With faith in immortality, it is easy to hold to the optimistic view that no day is wasted, though it is wrought with mistakes: It is used in the journey, and when twilight comes, you are one day nearer home.

Today is yours for you to use; and when it is over — good or bad — camp for the night; and at the dawn, pack up and move on, trusting, believing, never losing sight of your destination.

Your livelihood and comforts along the way are important, but not nearly as important as the faith that sustains you in your pilgrimage. This confidence makes life meaningful.

One sweetly solemn thought
Comes to me o'er and o'er;
I am nearer home today
Than I ever have been before.

—Phoebe Cary
1824 - 1871

Man goeth to his long home, and the mourners go about the streets.—Ecclesiastes 12:5

A FRIEND TO FRIENDS

Treat your friends as friends should be treated: be sincere, considerate, courteous, truthful, loyal, sympathetic and helpful. If you are a friend, you will stay when others walk out; you will lend a hand when others fold theirs.

It takes time to make and hold friends; for relationships made fast seldom last. The cannibal who eats you up the first time he sees you will just as quickly become nauseated with you later.

Hold your friend close, but grant him freedom. Don't stifle him — let him breathe — for true friendship cannot survive when one is so smothered there is no free breathing.

A friend is, as it were, a second self.

—*Cicero*
106 - 43 B.C.

Thine own friend, and thy father's friend, forsake not.—Proverbs 27:10

THE ANSWER IS IN YOU

You! you! what's in you is the answer to your problems. Outside help, but no outside solution. The solution has to come from within. It is more important to become and be than to get and possess. What you carry inside yourself will take you farther than what carries you. The mind builds barriers or demolishes them.

Helen Keller definitely proved this. She came into the world with a ravelled life, but she unravelled it. Born blind, deaf and mute, she was graduated with honors at Radcliffe. Her unconquerable spirit triumphed over all handicaps and lifted her to a place of glory.

> *You are not thrown to the winds, you gather certainly and safely around yourself! yourself! yourself! forever and ever.*
>
> —*Walt Whitman*
> 1819 - 1892

Our heart is not turned back.—Psalms 44:18

APPLY YOURSELF

If anything turns up, ordinarily you will have to do the turning; and in most cases it requires more initiative than ability.

Mediocrity wins over superiority when it is used and superiority isn't.

A little talent and much application excel on most jobs. You don't have to have the most talent to win, but you do have to use it more. Short legs win over long legs provided you move them faster.

This leaves the road to success open to all — a little harder for some, but it is open.

In this world and in every-day affairs, you have got to run fast merely to stay where you are; and in order to get anywhere you have got to run twice as fast as that.

—Woodrow Wilson

The King's business required haste.
— I Samuel 21:8

HINDERED BUT NOT DEFEATED

When the renowned Paganini's favorite violin was broken, he challenged the loss. Disappointed but not defeated, he got another one. "I will show them that the music is in me and not in any instrument," he avowed.

The way a person meets the tests of life determines his fate. What makes a cynic is thwarted hopes mishandled. When one's plans have to be altered, he runs the risk of building up frustrations which harden into bitterness and cynicism. But there is no reverse that cannot be turned to some good. And there is no breakage of material things that can stop the melody of life.

Men's best successes come after their disappointments.
—*Henry Ward Beecher*
1813 - 1887

We are perplexed, but not in despair.
—II Corinthians 4:8

NEVER GET BITTER

Never allow bitterness to sour your personality. No matter how hateful and heartless your circumstances may be, offset them with goodness.

Bitterness attracts bitterness and then multiplies by feeding on itself. It has a way of running to those who already have the most of it. But it shuns those with the greatest love and the highest degree of culture.

Trying to justify himself, the embittered person insists that he has cause for his condition. Maybe. Maybe not. Everybody has to drink from life's cup of bad breaks, but some have enough sweetness on the inside to dilute it — the bitter person didn't.

> *From the heart of this fountain of delight wells up some bitter taste to choke them even amid the flowers.*
>
> —*Lucretius*
> 99 - 55 B.C.

> The heart knoweth his own bitterness.
> — Proverbs 14:10

NEGATIVISM

Negation can negate you into nothing. Only the positive approach inspires the effort and releases the energy necessary to make a dynamic personality of achievement. Strong affirmatives give spirit, vitalize drive and attract friends.

Prophets of doom are not in demand. The negative outlook is unpleasant, unhelpful and unproductive. Negativism sees bad where there is good. This repels would-be friends and defeats attainable success.

A dog will bark against what he thinks is bad when it could be the approach of a new-found friend. A negative bark and a cynical growl will never make you the pet of the neighborhood.

Clear your mind of can't.

—*Samuel Johnson*
1709 - 1784

The Lord is the strength of my life; of whom shall I be afraid?—Psalms 27:1

UNITY REQUIRES LIKENESS

Nothing really unites people except agreement. The only genuine unity is found in like minds. It is awfully hard for our bodies to walk together when our minds run in opposite directions. A group may seem to be united, which is nothing more than lip union with divided hearts.

Union without harmony of minds can be like a violin without a violinist — no discord, but no music either; or it may be like an off-key squeaky fiddle in an orchestra — sooner or later it must be tuned or they stop playing. Union without unison is unsatisfactory. Pleasant togetherness demands compatibility of views.

> *Birds in their little nests agree;*
> *And 'tis a shameful sight,*
> *When children of one family*
> *Fall out, and chide, and fight.*
>
> —*Isaac Watts*
> 1674 - 1748

Can two walk together, except they be agreed?—Amos 3:3

DON'T BE TAKEN IN

Nothing nauseates like swallowed deceit. Please don't pass us anymore. Though we have had our fill, we might take another helping. Why? For the same reason Eve did — it looks good; and, we admit, most of us are not as clever as we think we are, not as discerning as we should be.

Surely some pointers are in order: Be wary. Investigate. Talk it over. Think it over. Pray over it. Sleep on it. Chew on it, but don't swallow until you are completely satisfied that it is nutritious and digestible. For nothing is as hard to keep down as sucker bait.

> *For of all the hard things to bear and grin,*
> *The hardest is being taken in.*
>
> *—Phoebe Cary*
> 1824 - 1871

Did I not say, Do not deceive me?
— II Kings 4:28

BE BRIEF

Life is too brief for man to be superfulous in his communications. Some reports which cover pages could be written on a cigarette paper. They remind me of a parrot that talked and talked and with all due respect to him. I had two criticisms: he was so repetitious and incoherent.

Brevity requires thinking, and this is no ordinary quality. The world's masterpieces of literature are brief: The Lord's Prayer of Example, sixty-six words. The Ten Commandments, reading time one minute. Lincoln's Gettysburg Address, about half a page.

Briefly concluded, that which takes too long to say, save it for eternity.

Brief let me be.
　　　　　　　　　　—William Shakespeare
　　　　　　　　　　1564 - 1616

... for they think that they shall be heard for their much speaking —Matthew 6:7

BURY THOSE WORRIES

If we could bury worry, we wouldn't have so many other funerals. Thus, let us consider some ways to put an end to one of the world's major killers — worry:

- Solve your problems rather than fret over them. Get expert advice, which can help you to temper anxiety into concern.
- Look ahead, not back, for there is plenty of everything up the line.
- Dismiss from your mind every disturbance that cannot be righted.
- While you realistically assess difficulty, have the habit of looking long at all of its possibilities for success.
- And lastly, meet your problems only as they arise, for each day has enough of its own.

Sing away sorrow, cast away care.

—*Miguel de Cervantes*
1547 - 1616

And take heed to yourselves, lest at any time your hearts be overcharged with . . . cares of this life . . .—Luke 21:34

ONE-WAY RELIGION

Religion to some people is like a sore thumb — always getting in their way. Some wisely change their behavior; others give up their religion; and many more suffer the conflicting pulls. The latter two reactions remind us of the little girl who closed her evening prayer by saying, "Goodby, God; I'm going to town tomorrow."

But the very nature of religion is incompatible with total abandonment or half embrace. If you feel frustrated and disorganized, pull yourself together by going one way. More commitment will resolve the divided heart and set both feet in one path.

Measure not men by Sundays, without regarding what they do all the week after.

—Thomas Fuller
1608 - 1661

If any man will come after me, let him deny himself, and take up his cross, and follow me.—Matthew 16:24

LYING REQUIRES TOO MUCH

It would be better to spit in a man's face than to slip a lie in his ears — better for both.

Aside from the fact that telling a falsehood depraves the teller and deceives the told, it is just too bothersome. You can tell the truth and forget it, but a lie keeps making demands. The naked truth needs no fig leaves to hide it, while a lie is in constant need of more clothing. The task goes on and on.

A lie looks like a little convenience for the perpetrator, but it requires more cunning and a better memory than the liar has; so, he loses.

Dare to be true: nothing can need a lie:
A fault, which needs it most, grows two thereby.

—*George Herbert*
1593 - 1633

He that speaketh lies shall not escape.
— Proverbs 19:5

BRAGGING

When I was a boy in the country, we had a mighty little rooster that was a mighty big crower. Finally when we got tired of it and took him to market, he was priced according to his weight rather than his noise and wing-flapping. Crowing doesn't bring anything in any market. No wonder, for it is all noise, not being, not doing.

As George Eliot said, "An ass may bray a good while before he shakes the stars down." Bragging never accomplishes anything, not even in prayer. Lo, all our boasting today will be but nought tomorrow. How frantic! How vain! How futile!

Do you wish people to think well of you? Don't speak well of yourself.

—*Blaise Pascal*
1623 - 1662

For before these days rose up Theudas, boasting himself to be somebody.—Acts 5:36

BE A MAN

A man ought to be a man. If he succeeds in this, he becomes the victor in the battle of his heart. Just anybody can lose and be a playful child, or a cry baby, or a bondsman to his appetites, or a slave to public opinion, or a spongy loafer. But only strong characters can put down the menial urges.

There are two selves who struggle within you; if the good self comes out on top, you have distinguished yourself. You have fought and won your manliness. And that makes you a man.

I mean to make myself a man; if I succeed at that, I shall succeed in everything else.

—James Abram Garfield
1831 - 1881

Gird up now thy loins like a man; for I will demand of thee, and answer thou me.
—Job 38:3

NO USE TO COMPLAIN

It has been said that the wheel which squeaks the loudest gets the most grease. Yes, but only for a time; after awhile it is discarded for a new wheel.

The habitual complainer soon loses his effectiveness.

Dogs growl, horses neigh and some people beef — frankly, I had rather listen to the dogs and horses.

Adjustment to what you cannot change is much more profitable than complaining about it. Changers and adapters — not complainers — lead our world. Grumbling about the weather will not change it, but you can change your clothes to fit it. And that's living!

It is no use to grumble and complain;
It's just as cheap and easy to rejoice,
When God sorts out the weather and sends rain —
Why, rain's my choice.

—James Whitcomb Riley

And when the people complained, it displeased the Lord.—Numbers 11:1

NAMES FOR FATHER

A father may be designated by various appelations: if he is wealthy and prominent — "Father"; or if he tills the soil — "Pa"; or if he sits in shirt sleeves, with open collar, at ball games — "Pop"; or if he has a special talent for carrying bundles meekly — "Papa" with the accent on the first syllable; or if he is a reformer in our society — "Papa" with the accent on the last syllable; or if he is a genuine pal to his children — "Dad."

But no matter what you call him, in most cases he is the embodiment of all these characteristics, and to his children he is the greatest.

Reverence and cherish your parents.

—Thomas Jefferson
1743 - 1826

Honor thy father and mother, which is the first commandment with promise.
—Ephesians 6:2

FATHER'S GREATEST JOB

Training his children is the world's highest calling for any man. Gravest responsibilities. Greatest possibilities. For in teaching the better principles, father develops in his children the better character.

The best children, like the prettiest flowers and the sweetest music, are made by cultivation. The most fragrant flowers do not grow wild. The most enrapturing music does not just happen. And the sweetest youth does not grow up pampered by parents and directed by self. It takes the dedicated mind and the determined hand of cultivation to bring out the best. And here the wise father performs his greatest job.

> *We are all blind until we see*
> *That in the human plan*
> *Nothing is worth the making if*
> *It does not make the man.*
>
> —*Edwin Markham*

My son, hear the instruction of thy father.—Proverbs 1:8

FATHER DOES WHAT HE MUST

Father has a heart that loves, rejoices, bleeds and breaks like that of a woman, though he may labor to withhold the visible signs. His role, which calls for firmness, sternness and readiness for life's battles, may dim his softness; for he has to go out into the world of cold conflict and struggle to strive for those he loves.

Taking life's beatings without tears or complaints, grimly and steadily carrying on, fighting and toiling as he takes the reproaches and praises with the same smiling face and unchecked determination, rough and ready — father has a heart of gold, though the world often fails to see it.

I like the man who faces what he must,
With steps triumphant and a heart of cheer;
Who fights the daily battle without fear.

—Sarah Knowles Bolton

For my father fought for you and adventured his life far, and delivered you out of the hand of Midian.—Judges 9:17

FATHER GETS SCHOOLED

Being a father is a schooling. It is an education to bear a child, provide for, train and educate him or her, and with anxiety of soul take the boy into your heart or hold that girl to your bosom, watching with eyes that never sleep and with a foresight that never slumbers.

The father's verbal teaching and careful example, his living hope and the sharing of that expectation, his dauntless courage and the instilling of that grit in the heart of the youngster — these teach the child, but also the father. For there is nothing that educates the parent like the child.

God has his small interpreters
The child must teach the man.

—John Greenleaf Whittier
1807 - 1892

Thou therefore which teachest another, teachest thou not thyself?—Romans 2:21

FATHER'S CARE RE-ENACTED

Nature's law of recompense is not faulty. The child must be protected. Years of care are necessary for the offspring to grow into manhood or womanhood. And during this time in which the world looks easy to youth, it is dealing the father strong opposition, serious setbacks and staggering blows.

Sons and daughters may not know this until the old man is dead and gone, but — they will learn. For by and by they will have children of their own, and the drama will be re-enacted. This time, however, the son who received has become the father and now divides his living with his own.

Doing, with courage stern and grim,
The deeds that his father did for him,
This is the line that for him I pen,
Only a dad, but the best of men.

—Anonymous

And he divided unto them his living.
—Luke 15:12

FATHER THE HERO

We esteem father because of his heroism. His sweat and tears and blood shed for us testify to his heroic nature; for he who struggled for others when the easy way was to run is a hero, call him what you will. We were protected by his daily bravery.

The highest and noblest sacrifice is "that a man may lay down his life for another." Father did this — not in one supreme gift, but in giving of himself little by little, day by day. The daily conflicts of earning a living and heading a household brought out the slumbering qualities of the hero.

Not at the battle front merit of in story,
Not in the blazing wreck, steering to glory;
Not while in martyr-pangs soul and flesh sever,
Died he — this Hero now; hero forever.

—Dinah Maria Mulock Craik

And we said unto my lord, We have a father ... — Genesis 44:20

FATHER'S GRIEF

"My son, my son, would God I had died for thee" are the moving and emotional words which have been uttered by countless fathers through the ages.

Those words have been spoken in hospital rooms as the child slipped down through the valley of the shadow of death. That wailing cry has been heard in the silent cities of the dead as broken-hearted fathers tenderly and sobbingly, yet heroically, expressed their bleeding sorrow.

The qualities of his heart seem to be a thousand hearts — each an absolute necessity to fatherhood — and in this instance a heart of grief.

That 'tis a common grief
Bringeth but slight relief;
Ours is the bitterest loss,
Ours is the heaviest cross;
And forever the cry will be,
"Would God I had died for thee,
O Absalom, my son!"

—Henry Wadsworth Longfellow
1807 - 1882

O my son Absalom! my son, my son Absalom! would God I had died for thee, O Absalom, my son, my son!—II Samuel 18:33

STRENGTHENED BY CONVICTION

The strength of a man is the strength of his convictions. He has to be sold before he can do a selling job. He has to believe in a thing before he is ready to stand for it.

Conviction refuses to court popularity, defies opinion. And when conviction costs, no matter how much, the price is paid with the feeling that right is being done.

The most noble souls have always had convictions coupled with courage. Their convictions were stronger than their fears. Their belief was a compelling power that lifted their voices, raised their hands and moved their feet. They believed! And they stood!

> *The only faith that wears well and holds its color in all weather is that which is woven of conviction . . .*
>
> —*James Russell Lowell*
> 1819 - 1891

So will I go in unto the king . . . and if I perish, I perish.—Esther 4:16

THE CLOCK REBUKES

While we complain of a lack of time, most of us have much more of it than we wisely use. Much of life is wasted in much ado about nothing.

We ought to learn from just looking at the clock's moving hands. What a forceful, though monotonous voice! Tick! Tick! Tick! They cry out that time is fleeting. They warn us not to waste man's scarcest commodity — time. They exhort us to move on, appropriating the stuff that life is made of — time.

There are no precious earthly values except life and time, and one cannot be separated from the other.

> *The clock upbraids me with the waste of time.*
>
> *—William Shakespeare*
> 1564 - 1616

So teach us to number our days, that we may apply our hearts unto wisdom.—Psalms 90:12

SOILED BY MUD WE THROW

Some people go around digging up dirt and slinging mud. But never — never — meet dirt with dirt. If you do, you will soon be spending most of your time wiping off mud and throwing it back.

Slinging mud at anyone generally shows that he has considerable cleanness; otherwise why try to smear him? The blackguards are already blackened.

There are worse things than being splattered with the hater's mud — one is to throw it back. Mudslinging dirties the slinger more than the target. And knowing this, the public soon reaches around those dirty hands to shake with the person who kept his clean.

Knowing, what all experience serves to show,
No mud can soil us but the mud we throw.

—*James Russell Lowell*
1819 - 1891

Recompense to no man evil for evil.
—Romans 12:17

FAULTFINDING REFLECTS SELF

A vulture will fly over a sweet-scented flower garden to seize a stinking carion.

In like manner, the critic passes over many beautiful qualities in search of a fault. He has developed the habit. His captious eyes have warped his view. His satisfaction comes from assailment.

The faultfinder is never a favorite. He is not appreciated. No statue is ever erected to him. The world knows his judgment of others is only a reflection of his own state, that he has a knocking fist instead of a helping hand, and that he would serve a better cause if he would change his ways and be a model.

Such as everyone is inwardly, so he judgeth outwardly.
—Thomas Kempis
1380 - 1471

For wherein thou judgest another, thou condemnest thyself.—Romans 2:1

HOLD THAT TEMPER

It's never good to strike while the head is hot. Steel loses its sharpness when it loses its temper, and so does man.

Anybody can lose his temper. Not hard at all. But to become angry at the right time, for the right purpose, in the right way, and in the right degree — now that is holding temper, and that is not easy.

But the bigger the person the more strength he has to hold what would be ungovernable urges within smaller and weaker people. The man with the big top, loaded with coolness, rationality and tolerance, doesn't blow it quickly.

A little pot boils quickly.

—*Dutch Proverb*

Let every man be swift to hear, slow to speak, slow to wrath.—James 1:19

ANSWER TO CALUMNY

The good hunting dog does not spend all his time hunting fleas. Neither does the accomplished person. If you run down all innuendos and misrepresentations, you won't have time to get on a trail that leads to anywhere worthwhile.

The best answer to calumny is to do your duty and say nothing. The evil that people hear about you proves nothing, and they recognize it, but what they see and hear for themselves they know.

The truth doesn't spread as fast as a lie, but it is weightier when it gets there. Eventually it will outweigh all rumors.

Life would be a perpetual flea hunt if a man were obliged to run down all the innuendos, inveracities, insinuations, and misrepresentations which are uttered against him.

—Henry Ward Beecher
1813 - 1887

Lead me, O Lord, in thy righteousness because of mine enemies; make thy way straight before my face. For there is no faithfulness in their mouth.—Psalms 5:8, 9

HANDLING TEMPTATION

We gain the strength of the temptation we withstand. Every person should make up his mind that he is bigger than the temptation which is trying to down him. If he does, he will get bigger as he stands. If he doesn't, he will get smaller as he falls.

Learn what your temptations are, and you will know what you are. This self-discovery will give an insight to the weaknesses you need to work on the hardest. For it is better to recognize the fire than to try to cure burnt fingers.

Resist! For the course of least resistance makes both rivers and men crooked.

More skillful in self-knowledge, even more pure,
As tempted more; more able to endure,
As more exposed to suffering and distress.

—William Wordsworth
1770 - 1850

My brethren, count it all joy when ye fall into divers temptations; knowing this, that the trying of your faith worketh patience.
— James 1:2, 3

WHEN CRITICIZED

You could not avoid criticism if you were a corpse, said nothing, did nothing. It will come.

Though disapproval deflates, it can be helpful. If one errs, criticism can point him to the better way. If without erring he is criticized, even that can help him to avoid the error in the future; furthermore, it can mellow him into being less critical of others.

It is our reaction to faultfinding — not what others say to us or about us — that blesses or hurts us. You can't help what some eyes *see* in you, but you can help what *is* in you.

When men speak ill of thee, live so nobody may believe them.
> —*Plato*
> 428 - 348 B.C.

Not rendering evil for evil, or railing for railing.—I Peter 3:9

HELP THE ERRING

There are shortcomings everywhere. No question about that. The question is: What shall our attitude be toward the blemished?

Shall we be sympathetic or scornful? Shall we lift them up or tread them down? As you answer, remember: Your attitude toward them will determine their attitude toward you. No person will look up to you, if you look down on him. The holier-than-thou attitude is much more fanciful than factual; it's too unrealistic to command respect.

As members of the human family, all err; and when one falls for the Tempter's bait, he needs the help of others to release him from the snare.

> *Revile him not, the Tempter hath*
> *A snare for all;*
> *And pitying tears, not scorn and wrath,*
> *Befit his fall.*
>
> —*John Greenleaf Whittier*
> 1807 - 1892

Brethren, if a man be overtaken in a fault, ye which are spiritual, restore such a one in the spirit of meekness; considering thyself, lest thou also be tempted.—Galatians 6:1

ACHIEVEMENT

Achievement! real achievement! consists of much:

— Self-command to turn on a day when it begins; self-discipline to turn it off when it ends.
— Courage to accept a challenge, and the grit to persevere.
— Determination to do what others think is impossible.
— Admiration of the good wherever it is found.
— Will to change what shouldn't be accepted; adjustment to accept what can't be changed.
— Knowledge of self and honesty to face it.
— Friendliness that causes a dog to wag his tail.
— Gentleness that beckons a child to run after you.
— And, lastly, the joy that comes from a glass of cold water, a delicious meal and a good bed.

What quality went to form a man of achievement.
—*John Keats*
1795 - 1821

Saul and Jonathan were lovely and pleasant in their lives . . . they were swifter than eagles, they were stronger than lions.
—II Samuel 1:23

LIVE NOW

Let today be mine, for I might not see tomorrow. May I take time to live before time takes me. The silver thread of life is too fragile to forfeit today for tomorrow. No one knows how much of his life is spent; but this he knows: each day there is a little less.

As Longfellow said, "The young may die, but the old must." Thus the wisest program for living and dying is to make your plans as if you would trod the earth for a thousand years and so walk as if you would take the last step today.

Live now, believe me, wait not till tomorrow;
Gather the roses of life today.

—Pierre de Ronsard
1524 - 1585

There is but a step between me and death.
— I Samuel 20:3

I AM AN OPTIMIST

The nurturing of Father Time should make man the child of optimism. The passing years ought to have given us the hopeful disposition.

There have been many more victories than defeats. Most problems were not as hard as they seemed, and most difficulties worked out better than we expected. We never rolled and tumbled through a night that didn't end; nor witnessed a storm that didn't pass; nor traveled a rough road that didn't turn.

So, hopefully, take off your gray-brown glasses and see the world as it is: The earth is turning and the sun is shining — and you are alive!

> *Take short views, hope for the best, and trust in God.*
> —*Sydney Smith*
> 1771 - 1845

I have been young, and now am old; yet have I not seen the righteous forsaken, nor his seed begging bread.—Psalms 37:25

PRESERVING DEMOCRACY

On this Fourth of July let us rededicate ourselves to the proposition that the people can be trusted to govern themselves. Let us resolve anew that this hallowed concept, bathed in the blood of heroic men and washed in the tears of courageous women, shall not perish by fault or default.

For democracy's success rests with the people: statehood on manhood, political self-government on personal self-government, national greatness on personal greatness, and liberty for all on restraint for each. Freedom's preservation truly lies in its true purpose: not the freedom to do wrong which hurts others, but the freedom to do right which helps all.

Liberty exists in proportion to wholesome restraint.
—*Daniel Webster*
1782 - 1852

Righteousness exalteth a nation: but sin is a reproach to any people.—Proverbs 14:34

RATHER BE RIGHT

Henry Clay, one of America's most eloquent statesmen, had just proposed a political gesture to an associate.

"It will ruin your prospects for the Presidency," was the lightning response of his friend.

But just as quickly, Mr. Clay commented, "I had rather be right than President."

Switching the tags of right and wrong might have switched some votes, but not the right of right and the wrong of wrong. It would have only disqualified him.

No matter what other qualifications one has, he can never be the right person for any job unless he does right.

The great man does not think beforehand of his words that they may be sincere, nor of his actions that they may be resolute — he simply speaks and does what is right.

—Mencius
372 - 289 B.C.

Woe unto them that call evil good, and good evil; that put darkness for light, and light for darkness; that put bitter for sweet, and sweet for bitter.—Isaiah 5:20

ME INSTEAD OF PEDIGREE

Not your ancestors, but you! Only you can make today yours! Good days are not found in the blood line, but in the line of duty. Who does something glorious for his descendants has no need for glorious ancestors.

It is better to have freedom than a line of kings in your ancestry; being free, you can rise to a place of recognition.

As you consider the family tree, don't forget that present fruits are more important than buried roots. There is more distinction in giving your posterity cause to brag about their ancestors than for you to brag about yours.

It is indeed desirable to be well descended,
but the glory belongs to the ancestors.

—Plutarch
46 - 120 A.D.

And think not to say within yourselves, We have Abraham to our father.—Matthew 3:9

KEEP CONSCIENCE BLAMELESS

If you would have the unerring assurance that all is well, have a compass — conscience — that points you as you study God's chart.

If you would have the aid of the one voice that means more than all other human voices, keep the approving words of the inner man coming through loud and strong.

If you would have the most effective disciplinarian, find it in a sense of moral consciousness.

If you would have an inexhaustible source of refreshment for the day, awake each morning in harmony with yourself.

And if you would have the softest pillow for the night, sleep with a soft heart.

A memory without a blot or contamination must be an inexhaustible source of pure refreshment.
—Charlotte Bronte
1818 - 1848

For our rejoicing is this, the testimony of our conscience . . .—II Corinthians 1:12

CAUSE AND EFFECT

Life must be lived under the unyielding law of cause and effect. Every effect has its cause. Comply with the rule and I shall be happy; violate it and I shall suffer.

It is about time we were learning the futility of trying to cure effects without remedying the causes.

The successful people in this world of sowing and reaping are smart enough to see the causes of things and strong enough to alter them. If we are successful, efficient and happy, it is no accident; it is the reaping from the sowing.

> *Happy is he who has succeeded in learning the causes of things.*
>
> *—Virgil*
> 70 - 19 B.C.

...for whatsoever a man soweth, that shall he also reap.—Galatians 6:7

TESTED LIKE A TREE

The wind tests the trees. Only the strong ones withstand the force. The decayed and rotten ones crack and break under the strain.

The way a strong and heroic person withstands trials and afflictions reminds us of a tree planted by the rivers of water, which has deep unseen strength, for it is deep-rooted and well grounded. The ravaging storms sweep over it, the biting frosts creep round it, but it keeps on standing, producing fruit. So it is with some people. They possess a deep, unseen power that is adequate for every trouble. Their hidden strength sustains them in the storms that break others.

> *Where the willingness is great, the difficulties cannot be great.*
> —*Niccolo Machiavelli*
> 1469 - 1527

> And he shall be like a tree planted by the rivers of water.—Psalms 1:3

NOT EXCUSED BY TROUBLE

You have troubles? Of course you do. And so does everybody else.

But they will be fewer and easier, if you meet them with the brave determination: *Come when you will, trial and trouble, nature's appointed powers of discipline and refinement, I am ready for the challenge.*

Trials have their compensations. Our world of difficulties was not designed to discourage and defeat, but to provide strength by conflict and melody by opposition. The oak grows strong by facing the opposing winds and the brook makes its music by running over the rocks. Nature accepts no difficulty. Neither does history.

> *Difficulty is the excuse history never accepts.*
> —*Samuel Grafton*

Thou, which hast showed me great and sore troubles, shall quicken me again, and shall bring me up again from the depths of the earth.—Psalms 71:20

REDUCING HARDSHIPS

Hardship comes to all, but it has a preference for the intemperate, the foolish, the fearful, the idler and the quitter. Oh, how hardship likes their company, so much that it stays with them.

But it doesn't like to associate long with the brave, the industrious, the believing and the wise; for they wrestle with it and overcome it. Trouble knocks them down occasionally, but they have a way of getting back up one step closer to better things. As victors, the blows knock them only toward grandeur.

To overcome difficulties is to experience the full delight of existence.

—*Arthur Schopenhauer*
1788 - 1860

Though I walk in the midst of trouble, thou wilt revive me.—Psalms 138:7

ABSTINENCE GETS EASIER

Abstinence comes easier with use. Its secret is found in refraining the present moment. Through use we develop power to resist or tendency to succumb. Triumph this moment, and the next is easier; fail, and the next is harder to win. For **nature's** rules cannot be mocked.

Overindulgence demands overpay, and will sooner or later collect. But abstinence is a benefactor with many professions — financier, physician, psychiatrist and minister — which gives money for the pocket, health for the body, clearness for the head, and peace for the heart.

It's you in control!

> *Refain to-night,*
> *And that shall lend a kind of easiness*
> *To the next abstinence: The next more easy;*
> *For use almost can change the stamp of nature.*
>
> —*William Shakespeare*
> 1564 - 1616

Abstain from all appearance of evil.
— I Thessalonians 5:22

TO TRY IS SUCCESS

For today to be mine, I need some goals though I reach them not. If they should elude my striving and grasping, I shall get more out of this day for trying.

There is such a thing as the paradox of achievement in nonfulfillment. If my working and praying do not bring me up to my aims, think how much lower I shall sink if I do not strive. So while I'm trying, I'm succeeding though I seem to fail. And come tomorrow I can try again. And that will be another success.

For thence — a paradox
Which comforts while it mocks —
Shall life succeed in that it seems to fail;
What I aspired to be,
And was not, comforts me;
A brute I might have been, but would not
sink i' the scale.
                              —*Robert Browning*
                              1812 - 1889

Hold up my goings in thy path, that my footsteps slip not.—Psalms 17:5

REPUTATION VERSUS CHARACTER

Reputation is the name you have — not necessarily the character you are. It is what people think of you — not always what you know yourself to be.

It glories in a world of vanities. And how vain a false reputation is! As Josh Billings stated, it can be obtained by giving publicly and stealing privately.

Reputation, of course, is valuable — a big asset — but character is priceless. A good reputation is only good business capital, but good character is goodness. The former can be obtained undeservedly or taken away without real cause, but the latter is left up entirely to you ... only you can build it or destroy it.

Reputation is an idle and most false imposition; oft got without merit, and lost without deserving.
—William Shakespeare
1564 - 1616

I know thy works, that thou hast a name that thou livest, and art dead.—Revelation 3:1

TRUST PROVIDENCE

Our trust in Providence gives assurance for to-day and anticipation for tomorrow. It takes the fear and dread out of life. Even the clouds reflect a goodness and the night conveys a peace.

Trust says, "Take a step, another, and another," and on we go — planting crops, building houses, expanding business, entering school, switching jobs — looking to the dawn. We make plans. We strive to carry them out. We do the best we can for ourselves and trust God for the rest. Life is a benediction. The days are ours — and so are the nights.

Heaven trims our lamps while we sleep.

—Amos Bronson Alcott
1799 - 1888

But I trusted in thee, O Lord; I said, Thou art my God. My times are in thy hand.—Psalms 31:14, 15

YOUR CHARACTER IS YOU

The strength of an individual lies in his character. Just as no building can stand out of proportion to its foundation, no life can stand out of measurement with its moral values. A weak character cannot support a strong life.

Character is not something you develop in a crisis; it's what you exhibit in a crisis . . . you had it all time.

Character is the accumulation of many thoughts and many deeds — not one. It's what you have become! You! You in the dark! And what you really are is the only basis for anything worthwhile.

A character is like an acrostic — read it forward, backword, or across, it spells the same.
—*Ralph Waldo Emerson*
1803 - 1882

If thou faint in the day of adversity, thy strength is small.—Proverbs 24:10

BE CAREFUL WITH CARES

Handle with care is my motto for handling life's cares; otherwise the cares will handle me and the day will be lost when it could be mine.

I need the interests of life, but must watch lest I become charged with anxiety, apprehension and worry.

Like roses, the concerns of life have their hidden thistles; and unless I deal with them discreetly, I shall be pricked without ever catching their fragrance.

Like taking passage on a plane, it is foolish to leave the baggage on my shoulders. It costs no more to lay the cares aside and relax.

Cast away care, he that loves sorrow
Lengthens not a day, nor can buy tomorrow.

—Thomas Dekker
1572 - 1632

And the care of this world, and the deceitfulness of riches, choke the word, and he becometh unfruitful.—Matthew 13:22

July 18

SUPPORT TRUTH

If you would find today tolerable and tomorrow tenable, give yourself unreservedly to truth. Falsehood may take the day, but not tomorrow. Only the truth outlasts the days.

The world may try to run off and leave the truth, but on the earth's completion of another cycle the unadorned realities will still be standing there and demanding that they be faced.

Truth is indestructible: club it, beat it, knife it, shoot it, strap it in the electric chair, but it refuses to die. It is immortal!

Truth, crushed to earth shall rise again;
The eternal years of God are hers;
But Error, wounded, writhes in pain,
And dies among his worshippers.

—William Cullen Bryant
1794 - 1878

I have chosen the way of truth.
— Psalms 119:30

PIETY PLUS

It's natural to find humanity in human beings. This means imperfection.

For one to effect over-piety puts his past under suspicion. The public is apt to come to the conclusion: Having committed all the sins there are, there is nothing left for this person but to exercise himself in pious horror as he laments in saintly tones the mistakes of others. So now in proud disdain he does refrain.

But there is no excellence in refusing to do that which one is tired of doing or no longer can do. What's virtue in a corpse can't be virtue in a live person.

> *Youth should heed the older-witted*
> *When they say, don't go too far —*
> *Now their sins are all committed,*
> *Lord, how virtuous they are!*
>
> *—Wilhelm Busch*

For all have sinned, and come short of the glory of God.—Romans 3:23

A DRESSED UP LIE

Dressing up a lie just makes a bigger lie. The ornaments add to the wrong — make it more attractive but more hurtful, for it is more deceptive.

Then why do men lie? Why do they clothe falsehood with more fabrications? They blindly think perversion will do more for them than truth. It is their crafty manner of acquisition. Their cunning form of equalization. Their supposed help in time of trouble.

But a lie can never be whitened by simply clothing it in white. A lie is a lie, dress it or undress it as you will.

A lie, turned topsy-turvy, can be prinked and tinseled out, decked in plumage new and fine, till none knows its lean old carcass.

—Henrik Ibsen

The lip of truth shall be established for ever: but a lying tongue is but for a moment.—Proverbs 12:19

BE SLOW IN GIVING UP THE OLD

It is always a new wonder how people can so easily reject that which is called old: old truths, old principles, old concepts, old slogans. Nothing is bad because it is old, and nothing is good because it is new.

Whatever has been so relevant as to outlast the ages deserves more than a hasty rejection. Look at the rubbish heaps of new ideas, painfully discarded and stacked higher and higher, before you remove the ancient landmarks. Those markers don't stand without purpose.

Though we call ageless truths old, actually they are younger than youth. That which defies time can never age.

The public doesn't require any new ideas. The public is best served by the good, old-fashioned ideas it already has.

—Henrik Ibsen

Remove not the old landmark.—Proverbs 23:10

THINK!

Think! for it distinguishes man — raises him above the animal and makes him more like God.

Think! for it is the greatest human power — harness it as you will.

Think! for no brain is stronger than its weakest think — and thought by thought man forges his chain of success.

Think! for it is your chief vocation — no matter how you earn your bread.

Think! for it will shorten your job — whatever it is.

Think! for it is more essential to living than education — and more pertinent to fruition than grammar.

When a thought takes one's breath away,
a lesson on grammar seems an impertinence.

—Thomas Wentworth Higginson

O Lord, how great are thy works! and thy thoughts are very deep.—Psalms 92:5

PRAYER FOR COURAGE

God, give me courage for this day. May I not turn coward before it's difficulties. May I prove equal to its duties. Come what will, let me cling to the philosophy that I am not beaten. Let me see myself not as a worm to crawl at men's feet, but as a man who holds up his head and stands tall in the midst of men. May I never bow to failure, and when a setback comes, let me see it as only an experience for a rematch. Knowing that fear is a lack of faith and vision, may I believe, lift up my eyes, and walk unafraid.

Nothing is as valuable to a man as courage.

—Terence
190 (?) - 159 (?) B.C.

Be of good courage, and let us play the men.—II Samuel 10:12

COOKING LASTS

It has been said that the best way to a man's heart is through his stomach. Maybe it is. Maybe it's not. But there is one thing sure — no woman can hold long a man's heart if his stomach growls.

When man provides the home and woman keeps it, he brings home the bacon and she cooks it, each can be proud of the other. This encourages mutual appreciation and dependence, which promote a love that lasts.

Though man is fond of love, he still says, "Three times a day, let's eat."

Kissing don't last: cookery do.

—George Meredith

She riseth also while it is yet night, and giveth meat to her household, and a portion to her maidens.—Proverbs 31:15

LET THE CHIPS FLY

In cutting wood, we can't worry too much about where the chips fall. No chips, no cutting, but no wood either. No offenses, no standing, but no man either.

A very famous woodcutter once said, "Stand with anybody that stands right while he is right and part with him when he goes wrong" — Abraham Lincoln.

Manhood asks: What is right? Not who is for it or against it. Observing where men stand on an issue only gauges popularity — a fickle thing — which comes and goes. But right is stable, and time and eternity are on the side of him who hews the line.

> *He will hew the line of right, let the chips fall where they may.*
>
> *—Roscoe Conklin*
> 1829 - 1888

And Asa did that which was right...
— I Kings 15:11

HYPOCRISY INDIRECTLY COMPLIMENTS

When a wolf puts on sheep's clothing, he compliments the sheep. Being two-faced indirectly condemns the first and praises the second.

So there is evidence of good everywhere, even in hypocrisy. The hypocrite pays tribute to refinement, grace, good manners, and religion, though his heart is not in them. He knows their value or he would not put on their masks and parade as something he is not.

Hypocrites should encourage rather than discourage you. They prove the reality of the thing they mimic, that it is something good to be.

Hypocrisy, detest her as we may,
May claim the merit still, — that she admits
The worth of what she mimics with such care,
And thus gives virtue indirect applause.

—William Cowper
1731 - 1800

Even so ye also outwardly appear righteous unto men, but within ye are full of hypocrisy, and iniquity.—Matthew 23:28

THE FORCE OF SILENCE

There are times when silence has the loudest voice. Occasions arise when the best way to say much is to say nothing. The eloquence of silence can be reprimanding, or consenting, or unanswerable, or persuasive, or peaceable. It can also be otherwise.

So, when do we speak and when do we refrain? The answers are an education in the School of Good Days: Say nothing when you have nothing to say, or when you have said enough, or when you don't know how to say it, or when it is the wrong time, or when it would hurt others, or when it would fall on deaf ears. This requires character.

Silence is one of the hardest arguments to refute.
>   —*Josh Billings*
>   1818 - 1885

And he answered him to never a word; insomuch that the governor marveled greatly.—Matthew 27:14

MORE THAN A LIVING

Mans owes it to himself to make more than a living — make his living worthwhile. It is not enough to live and learn — he should learn and live. A little learning can add a lot to living. When we learn that man's life consists not in the abundance of the things he possesses, we can do more living; we can live on less and enjoy it more.

The world owes you nothing — it was here first. You must earn your bread — and the right to enjoy it, which is accomplished through mental victories. You have life; what you do with it is your choice.

Now I am beginning to live a little, and feel less like a sick oyster at low tide.

—Louisa May Alcott
1832 - 1888

Live joyfully with the wife whom thou lovest all the days of the life of thy vanity, which he hath given thee under the sun, all the days of thy vanity: for that is thy portion in this life, and in thy labor which thou takest under the sun.—Ecclesiastes 9:9

GOLD'S VALUE EXAGGERATED

In this age of misplaced values, the package is prized beyond the contents, the clothes above the man, and the possessions more than the possessor.

The veil of gold owned by any family is expected to hide all its unseemliness — grandpa's backwoods origin, and grandpa's errant grandson and erratic granddaughter.

In the spirit of the times, if a man has a gold idol, there is no end to the long line of worshipers who come to fall down before it, and he may think they are paying homage to him; but let him lose the money, and see what happens to the line.

> *The advantages of wealth are greatly exaggerated.*
> —*Leland Stanford*

> **Your** gold and silver is cankered . . .
> — James 5:3

BE TACTFUL

A little tact will often prevent resistance. It has the discernment and judgment to approach opposition at the least sensitive point. It is the seeing eye, the hearing ear, the easy step and the soft touch. Diplomacy knows how to do things, and thus increases the chances of success a hundredfold. Obstacles are not knocked down; they are climbed over skillfully. It turns adverse circumstances into advantages.

Tact wins, because it has winning ways. Here is the formula: Be rationally right; be affably aggressive; be politely plain; be effortlessly emphatic; be patiently positive; be gracefully gentle.

Tact is the ability to remove the sting from a dangerous stinger without getting stung.

—James Bryce

A man hath joy by the answer of his mouth: and a word spoken in due season, how good is it!—Proverbs 15:23

DIFFICULTIES TRAIN US

Nothing in life is so hard but what we can make it easier by the way we meet it. Difficulties are the trainers which develop character. By strengthening ourselves to overcome trials, we add to our might. All hindrances are tests. They try the reality of our resolutions and the genuineness of our purposes.

The hot sun tries the roots of the plants. The strong wind proves the tree's branches. The high hill tests the car's motor. So it is with man: when life is uphill, his character and faith are being tested — and developed.

> *Difficulties are meant to rouse, not discourage. The human spirit is to grow strong by conflict.*
> —*William Ellery Channing*

For thou, O God, hast proved us: thou hast tried us, as silver is tried.—Psalms 66:10

BE PRACTICAL

No ambition can help any man unless he is practical. Set your eye on a star, but don't forget to see it from the down-to-earth view. That will strike a balance between vision and workability.

It's never good to have your head so high in the air you can't see where you are stepping; nor so low you can't see to reach above yourself. Some toe-stumping can be avoided by looking where you are going.

Adapting your life to practicality, step by step, may not be the most visionary, but it is the most fruitful.

A man gazing on the stars is proverbially at the mercy of the puddles on the road.

—Alexander Smith
1830 - 1867

The wise man's eyes are in his head; but the fool walketh in darkness.—Ecclesiastes 2:14

WHEN KNOCKED DOWN GET UP

Success requires you to get up just one more time than you get knocked down.

That's what life is: getting knocked down and getting up; stay down and you miss half of life — the half that makes the whole worthwhile.

The blow may be a swinging door, a harsh word, a lost job, a bad investment, a misplaced confidence, a lapse in health, or a loved one's passing.

Whatever fells you, get up. If it only staggers you, gain your balance and renew the struggle. Outlast the blows — that's the secret of triumph.

It is hard! But it is harder to lose!

When falls the hour of evil chance —
And hours of evil chance will fall —
Strike though with but a broken lance!
Strike, though you have no lance at all!

—Anonymous

Have not I commanded thee? Be strong and of a good courage; be not afraid, neither be thou dismayed.—Joshua 1:9

STAY YOUNG

It can be your fortune to stay young. You can avoid old age. You can! For age is only a quality of mind.

You are young if you:

— Have turned loose of yesterday.
— Enjoy today.
— Anticipate tomorrow.
— Look up when knocked down.
— Feel there is much to learn.
— Are ambitious.
— Are enthusiastic.
— Dream.
— Have no wrinkles on the heart.
— Feel young.

But —

> *If you have left your dreams behind,*
> *If hope is cold,*
> *If you no longer look ahead,*
> *If your ambition's fires are dead,*
> *Then you are old.*
>
> *—Anonymous*

How old art thou?—Genesis 47:8

IDEALS DIRECT DESTINY

Ideals are the basis for character, the motive for achievement and the direction for destiny.

Having been defined as good, ideals arouse one to reach them. They are the power to fashion and shape human lives. They are the blueprint of higher living. They are the urgings of the better self.

Ideals won't let you settle for the low in life; they keep you reaching. They won't let you make a truce with evil; they keep you on the side of right.

What a lift it is to have such ideals that you can't get even close to reaching them without being elevated.

> *Ideals are like stars; you will not succeed in touching them with your hands . . . choose them as your guides, and following them you will reach your destiny.*
>
> —*Carl Schurz*

I have walked in mine integrity: I have trusted also in the Lord; therefore I shall not slide.—Psalms 26:1

UTILIZING THE WHOLE MAN

Living is not a question of whether man shall partially function — that's settled, if he lives — but what about the full usage of his faculties? The intellect to search for deeper answers? The vision to see farther ahead? The heart to stick a little longer? The hands to tire less quickly? The feet to keep on climbing? The ears to hear sweeter melodies? The tongue to speak a kinder language — love? And his spirit to enjoy a superior fellowship — with God?

All of this adds up to achievement, which is more than ALMOST — it is! It is you! It is you utilized more fully!

What small potatoes we all are, compared with what we might be.

—*Charles Dudley Warner*
1829 - 1900

They go from strength to strength ...
— Psalms 84:7

TOO SMART TO LIE

It is neither right nor bright to lie. Its only hope of success is in keeping itself unknown. It can't stand investigation. And dealing in a trade that can't endure the light of day has a dark future.

A lie is a spectacle of hypocrisy deceitfully masquerading in the robes of integrity. Like a snake in the grass, it strikes. It is an infamous effort to cash in falsehoods, zigzags and broken promises. It makes human relationships a travesty and man's word a dagger in the mouth.

Goodness is too good to lie, and wisdom is too wise to do it.

For want of me the world's course will not fail:
When all its work is done, the lie shall rot;
The truth is great, and shall prevail,
When none cares whether it prevail or not.

—*Coventry Patmore*

The lip of truth shall be established for ever: but a lying tongue is but for a moment.—Proverbs 12:19

PLAYING BLIND TO EVIL

One of our personal deficiencies is to play blind to evil. The course of least resistance is to close our eyes to wickedness. It is less disturbing to see no danger. But it is unthinkable that man would walk off a cliff, telling himself it is not there; or after he has plunged a thousand feet to exclaim, "Everything is all right so far."

To close our eyes and stop our ears changes nothing.

The first step in reformation is the recognition of evil for what it is; the second is for it to become to us an insufferable wrong.

The world is grown so bad,
That wrens make prey where eagles
dare not perch.

—William Shakespeare
1564 - 1616

But evil men and seducers shall wax worse and worse, deceiving, and being deceived.
— II Timothy 3:13

CLIMB

The ladder of life has its splinters. As long as you ascend, you climb with the points; but look out, if you start to slip.

The great law of life is ascension. And in case you slip, pick out the splinters and keep climbing. There has never been a person up toward the top without splinter prints. It may sound trying and painful to climb two hours and pick splinters one hour, but to alternate one's efforts in such proportions will never see him at the bottom of the ladder.

Give me the heart to climb and when I slip to climb again.

> *I steadier step when I recall*
> *That, if I slip, Thou dost not fall.*
>
> —*Arthur Hugh Clough*
> 1819 - 1861

Hold up my goings in thy paths, that my footsteps slip not.—Psalms 17:5

CONSCIENCE GIVES COURAGE

No man is braver than his conscience. If his conscience condemns, everything is frightening; a mouse looks like a giant; and the night is always long and spooky. On the other hand, if he has the approval of self, he is more apt to be unafraid and undaunted as he faces the criticisms and condemnations of a misguided people.

The fearful cries of cowardice can be the self-made spooks of a hurting conscience; and conversely the fearless calls of true valor may be the amplified whisperings of an approving inner voice. So if you would keep your courage, keep your conscience.

My conscience hath a thousand several tongues,
And every tongue brings in a several tale,
And every tale condemns me for a villain.

—William Shakespeare
1564 - 1616

And they which heard it, being convicted by their own conscience, went out one by one.—John 8:9

BUSINESS AHEAD OF PLEASURE

An indispensable requisite of duty is that it be placed ahead of pleasure. The immaturity that causes one to abandon business for pleasure will wreck any hope of achievement.

Business success is very demanding — not acci: dental. It requires priority, thought, judgment, decision, daring, diligence, opportunity, work, drive, perseverance; but if you, in your pursuit of pleasure, relegate these necessities to secondary places, then you must take a back seat in the business world where there are fewer demands. It's sort of like sitting on the back pew at church — it requires less than the amen corner.

Don't let yourself be diverted from your duty until you have finished — not even if a cannon goes off at your elbow.

—Konrad Adenauer

And there was set meat before him to eat: but he said, I will not eat, until I have told mine errand.—Genesis 24:33

STRONGER THROUGH NECESSITY

Like the little birds, we are not going to fly until we get shaken out of our nests; nor shall we develop the strongest wings until we try them against the wind.

The dove in the fable, perturbed because the wind ruffled its feathers, thoughtlessly wished for a firmament void of air that it might dart through empty space like lightning. Foolish bird! For without that air it could neither soar nor live.

Brothers in struggle (and that's all of us), do not foolishly wish away every opposition. It is better to meet and master our difficulties that we can be lifted higher and made stronger through conflict.

Let the boy win his spurs.

—Edward III
1312 - 1377

For thou hast girded me with strength to battle.—II Samuel 22:40

THE BRAGGART

"I sure shook that bridge," said the mouse to the elephant after they had crossed it. So goes the brags of the self-praiser.

The only thing in his favor is he's not apt to have any rivals in praising himself. The world will let him have the floor on that subject. They think he must be a sham, or he wouldn't spend so much time talking himself up. The world appraises (not praises) him as an empty vessel, for he has those distinctive empty sounds.

If you want good things said about you, be praise-worthy and let others do it — not you.

An ass may bray a good while before he shakes the stars down.
—*George Eliot*
1819 - 1880

Let another man praise thee, and not thine own mouth; a stranger, and not thine own lips.—Proverbs 27:2

BOTTOMLESS CUP OF
SELF-RIGHTEOUSNESS

Self-righteousness is an ugly, bottomless cup; though the self-lover pours and pours, he is never able to fill it. Pouring himself into himself adds nothing. No wonder! For nothing plus nothing equals nothing.

He wants to look big, but goes at it backwards. He should have more interest in being than in seeming, and then he would humbly pour himself out of himself into the service of God and humanity. Now that adds something: real righteousness, wholeness of self. And that's what fills the cup.

God will fill my cup, but only if it is empty of pharisaical impurities.

God of the lily's cup,
Fill me! I hold this empty chalice up.

Frederic Lawrence Knowles
1869 - 1905

But we are all as an unclean thing, and all our righteousnesses are as filthy rags; and we all do fade as a leaf; and our iniquities, like the wind, have taken us away. —Isaiah 64:6

AIMING HITS FORTUNE

As man sets his aims he raises or lowers his standing. No man is apt to reach what he doesn't aim at. In the pursuit of aimlessness he is sure to find it — nothing!

In contradistinction, it is through purposes that he captures fortune, for he goes out to find it.

By aiming he marshals his forces: employs his talents, uses his time, harnesses his strength and directs his quest. With all this going for him, he is sure to go places he otherwise would not. And though he does not reach his goal, he finds achievement in purpose.

> *'Tis not what man does which exalts him,*
> *But what man would do.*
>
> —*Robert Browning*
> 1812 - 1889

> And, behold, I purpose to build a house unto the name of the Lord my God.
> —I Kings 5:5

BE ETHICAL

Strive mightily, but maintain the highest ethics in debating your cause. For you can win the argument and lose the person. Winning at any price is too big a price; for then you have lost. Winning is definitely not winning unless it is ethical.

Cutting your opponent's throat doesn't put a halo slightly above yours. Remember — cut-throats are not much in demand, for no one wishes to be abused. Unquestionably, you haven't triumphed unless you are in demand when you get through.

So, press your cause, prod it, propel it, push it, pull it, but don't forget to be friends to those who stand in the way.

> *And do as adversaries do in law,*
> *Strive mightily, but eat and drink as friends.*
>
> —*William Shakespeare*
> **1564 - 1616**

> Debate thy cause with thy neighbor himself.
> — Proverbs 28:9

SWEARING IS POOR COMMUNICATION

The man had nothing to say and he swore; maybe this is why — he had nothing to say. Another man had something to say and he swore; maybe this is why — he knew not how to say it. And another had something to say and he could have said it, but didn't; he swore, and maybe this is why — habit.

In all three cases, it was poor communication. Each wasted his breath in an unprofitable and abominable custom. Showing irreverence toward the Creator does not lend force to language, nor to personality; and it certainly does not manifest courtesy to others who have to listen.

To swear is neither brave, polite, nor wise.
You would not swear upon the bed of death:
Reflect! Your Maker yet may stop your breath.

—William Cowper
1731 - 1800

Thou shalt not take the name of the Lord thy God in vain.—Exodus 20:7

PRAYER DEFINED

What is prayer? The flight of man to the bosom of God. Infirmity leaning on Infinity. Misery wooing peace. The gathering together of inner resources. The unity of body, mind and spirit, which gives powerless man powerful strength. The key that unlocks the morning, and the bar that bolts the night.

It is a sure position which keeps man from standing in his own way. It is a natural impulse when the well runs dry, when the storm hits, and when the death angel hovers. It is the one place every child of God can go when all other places are closed.

Prayer is the simplest form of speech
That infant lips can try;
Prayer the sublimest strains that reach
The Majesty on high.

—*James Montgomery*
1771 - 1854

Unto thee, O Lord, do I lift up my soul.
— Psalms 25:1

THE EFFICACY OF PATIENCE

For more power, develop more patience. It can make a *Job* out of every one of us.

Patience hopes in sickness, purposes in prosperity, and holds on in poverty. It is unrestrained by intolerance, unmoved by reproach, unshaken by calumny, and unblended by persecution. It produces faithfulness in church, harmony in families, success in business, and magnanimity in society.

Patience controls the anger, bridles the tongue, and restrains the hand. It endures hardships, rides out the storm, picks up the pieces and builds anew. It sees a new day and awaits the dawn. It does too much not to be working for me.

Who bides his time — he tastes the sweet
Of honey in the saltest tear;
And though he fares with slowest feet
Joy runs to meet him drawing near.

—James Whitcomb Riley

Better is the end of a thing than the beginning thereof: and the patient in spirit is better than the proud in spirit.—Ecclesiastes 7:8

THE GOLDEN YEARS

Nature has a way of compensating man for the loss of youth; as the years come in which he must use his body less, experience has prepared him to use his mind more. As much as physical prowess is treasured, it is not comparable to intellectual competence.

The riper years can be the golden years: a time in which one can find blessedness in his own company, an accumulation of experiences which guard against phantoms, a maturity which has become fed up with youth's sucker bait, an unfoldment of more hindsight which gives deeper insight and longer foresight. Yes! They can be the best years!

Strike when thou wilt, the hour of rest,
But let my last days be my best.

—*John Greenleaf Whittier*
1807 - 1892

And they shall bring forth fruit in old age.
— Psalms 92:14

SWALLOW PRIDE

Some people have indigestion because they have trouble swallowing their pride. And if it were not so inflated, it would not be so hard to swallow. It's too big.

Don't confuse the issue: It's all right to hold up your head — you should — but do so without turning up your nose. Now it's the turned-up-nose group that is so proud of so little. They crave halos when they are not holy, chief seats when they are not leaders, honor when they are not honorable, and recognition while they hope what they are will not be recognized.

They have fed on the wrong stuff!

Upon what meat doth this our Caesar feed,
That he is grown so great?

—*William Shakespeare*
1564 - 1616

And man's pride shall bring him low: but honor shall uphold the humble in spirit.—
Proverbs 29:23

RELY ON SELF

If you would have, look to self. I have seen the prescript work in the lives of many. I knew a banker who went bankrupt, as many did, in the Great Depression. Undefeated, he began on foot to sell used clothing from house to house. Later he opened a used clothing and furniture store. Next he went into the oil business and became rich again.

The world awards its prizes to people of self-reliance. And so does God! Let self-dependence be a part of your religion; for, after all, God helps those who help themselves. No locked door will open for you unless you are the key.

If you would have a faithful servant,
and one that you like, serve yourself.

—Benjamin Franklin
1706 - 1790

She considereth a field; and buyeth it: with the fruit of her hands she planteth a vineyard.—Proverbs 31:16

AIM HIGH

It was the colorful P. T. Barnum, the circus king, who said, "If I shoot at the sun I may hit a star." We don't always reach our aims, but O how much higher we rise because we try. Attainment is no accident. Having no aim means no success. No aspiration grows leaden feet!

Every person is capable of raising himself; there are two requirements: first, look up and second, walk up. The higher your aim, in keeping with reality, the more transcendent you become; but aiming no higher than the alarm clock would help some people.

Greatly begin! though thou hast time
But for a line, be that sublime,
Not failure, but low aim, is crime.

—*James Russell Lowell*
1819 - 1891

Therefore we his servants will arise and build.—Nehemiah 2:20

GET GOOD ADVICE

It is easy to get advice. All you have to do is catch a cold. The trouble is: most of it is not worth very much. Comes free, but is still greatly overpriced. Now don't let this close your ears to counsel. Just be sure it is good!

It takes wisdom merely to seek wise advice, to know where to look and how to appraise it. Don't listen to the failures! Look elsewhere. Seek guidance from knowledgable men and women of experience and common sense. Then there is the problem of following it, which takes more than genius.

Advice is a drug in the market;
the supply always exceeds the demand.

—*Henry Wheeler Shaw*
(Josh Billings)
1818 - 1885

Every purpose is established by counsel: and with good advice make war.—Proverbs 20:18

SCHOOL OF AFFLICTION

Affliction is the school that lasts a lifetime; no one ever graduates until he steps all the way across the stage into the next world. Every person is a student; the courses vary with individuals, but each has his own load.

Painful and trying, no school does more for us, if we are apt learners. In every hurt, there can be a lesson that develops character, increases sympathy, adds to patience, fortifies for disappointment, firms will power, lifts the eyes to see the more valuable values, and multiplies wisdom by prodding one to think deeper.

Now, this personal question: What about your grades?

> *Know how sublime a thing it is to suffer and be strong.*
> —*Henry Wadsworth Longfellow*
> 1807 - 1882

> For our light affliction, which is but for a moment, worketh for us a far more exceeding and eternal weight of glory.
> —II Corinthians 4:17

YOU AND YOUR NEIGHBOR

In fulfilling your duty toward your neighbor, keep a pleasing manner and a smiling face. Strive to make yourself a source of pleasure to him. Be sincere. Be humble. Be encouraging. Be consoling. Follow after the things which make for peace. Conceal his faults and mistakes, remembering that you have yours. Express appreciation for the kindness he renders you. Compliment him, but don't flatter him. And when you err, as all humans do, never take it out on him — apologize. And last of all, as Benjamin Franklin said, ". . . don't pull down your hedge."

It is your concern when your neighbor's wall is on fire.
    —*Horace*
    65 - 8 B.C.

They helped every one his neighbor; and every one said to his brother, Be of good courage.
— Isaiah 41:6

OVERRATING THE PAST
HURTS THE PRESENT

It is not wise to minimize the present by maximizing the past. The past was good, but perhaps not as good as some would have us think. Its presently regarded excellency is not so much in blue-ribbon accomplishments as in an inclination to over appreciate it now because it was under appreciated then.

Furthermore, as man's future shrinks, there is a tendency to swell his past. This accounts for much of the praise heaped on yesteryears. While they were wonderful, most of the merit is in the mind. Accordingly, the realistic value of today is what each makes it.

> *That sign of old age, extolling the past at the expense of the present.*
>
> —*Sydney Smith*
> 1771 - 1845

> Say not thou, What is the cause that the former days were better than these? for thou dost not inquire wisely concerning this.
> —Ecclesiastes 7:10

BURY RUMORS

If all the rumors were true, surely none of us would be worth shooting; but all of us would be rich. There are rumors about people's sins, and there are rumors about "gold in them thar hills" — investments. But usually the gold is not there, and in most cases neither is the sin. If we can be fooled by believing in fool's gold, then can't we be bigger fools for believing every rumor about some person's frailty?

One of the fine things about a cemetery is it spreads no rumors. Why not have a cemetery just for rumors? Bury them! Deep!

Rumor is a pipe
Blown by surmises, jealousies, conjectures,
And of so easy and so plain a stop
That the blunt monster with uncounted heads
The still-discordant wavering multitude,
Can play upon it.

—*William Shakespeare*
1564 - 1616

Mischief shall come upon mischief, and rumor shall be upon rumor.—Ezekiel 7:26

LEAVE A BETTER WORLD

Each generation has the right to use the world, but not abuse it. The who-cares philosophy, which gets what you can, anyway you can, as long as you can, leaves a wasted world in its wake.

If our hands are thieves which snatch the wealth of ages; if our feet are block busters which trample nature's provisions; if we are a people whose sensitivity is seared to polluted streams, poisoned air, huge debts and dog-eat-dog morals, we are more than exploiters — we are culprits whose prodigality shall affect the unborn.

So let us ask: When we vacate this old world and the new tenants move in, what will they find?

It pays . . . to try and do things, to accomplish things in this life, and not merely to have a soft and pleasant time.

—Theodore Roosevelt

One generation passeth away, and another generation cometh: but the earth abideth for ever.—Ecclesiastes 1:4

PRAYER FOR CLEAN HANDS

O Lord, help me to keep my hands clean. May I have hands that never steal; hands that never take a bribe; hands that know no greed; hands that move when there is work to be done; hands that mind their own business; hands unsoiled with broken trusts; hands that never knife a friend in disloyalty; hands that never hold back any man; hands that never cheer when others fall; hands that are never raised in angry blows; hands unstained with the blood of the innocent; hands that are fit for the other fellow to shake.

> *Ring in the valiant man and free,*
> *The larger heart, the kindlier hand.*
>
> *—Alfred Tennyson*
> 1809 - 1892

The righteous also shall hold on his way, and he that hath clean hands shall be stronger and stronger.—Job 17:9

PROPAGANDA CAN MAKE
EVEN SATAN LOOK GOOD

Propaganda often is the prop for error. Indoctrination can change men's thinking, but not facts. You can whitewash wrong and brainwash man; but when you get through, neither has been laundered. You can't change the color of sin by calling it white.

Sugaring over the devil does not sweeten him — nor you; to try it, leaves bitterness in the mouth. For guile is always bitter, though a sugared piety is feigned. And to rid it, one must replace the acrid perversion with the sweet truth. This demands investigation, discernment and the necessary sacrifice to make the exchange.

With devotion's visage
And pious action we do sugar o'er
The devil himself.

—*William Shakespeare*
1564 - 1616

... wilt thou not cease to pervert the right ways of the Lord?—Acts 13:10

MORE PRECIOUS THAN RUBIES

Wisdom is priceless. This faculty is unquestionably high on the list of personal values. The Bible commends it; the philosophers praise it; the poets extol it; and the wise seek it.

Sir W. Temple said, "A man's wisdom is his best friend; folly, his worst enemy."

Defined, wisdom is the use of knowledge and experience in meeting successfully the circumstances of life. It puts ready hinges on the door of success and a soft glove on the fist of fate. Some call it common sense. Whatever it is, the wise get more of it; but fools, never.

A grain of gold will gild a great surface,
but not so much as a grain of wisdom.

—Henry David Thoreau
1817 - 1862

Wisdom . . . is more precious than rubies; and all the things thou canst desire are not to be compared unto her. Length of days is in her right hand; and in her left hand riches and honor. Her ways are ways of pleasantness, and all her paths are peace.
—Proverbs 3:13-17

THE GOOD TEACHER

Say all that man has ever said about a good teacher, and you won't say half enough. The great teacher gives more than ideas — ideals, more than facts — inspiration, more than cold answers — warm provocations to think, and more than a knowledge of the past — a challenge for the future.

She deals with the noblest work of God and man's only real value, which is man himself; for all other values, no matter how great they are, relate to him.

The excellent teacher makes the ideal teaching situation, no matter how many aids are lacking.

Give me a log hut, with only a simple bench, Mark Hopkins on one end and I on the other, and you may have all the buildings, apparatus and libraries without him.

—*James Abram Garfield*
1831 - 1881

And he began to teach them many things.
— Mark 6:34

THE IDLER

The lazy sluggard—that do-nothing with a warped mind who had rather suffer than work; that victim of a disease which shrinks giants into Pygmies; that wasteful liver of a sorry life; that sluggard left behind by an energetic world; that lengthening shadow of failure and dismay; that miserable creature who wakes to disinterest, eats to unhappiness, drinks to boredom, talks to dullness, sleeps to restlessness and passes his empty days in futile breathing; that child of mischief tutored by the naughty teacher nought; that key figure who — if "an idle mind is the devil's workshop" — could put the devil out of shop by going to work.

The idle mind knows not what it is it wants.

—*Quintus Ennius*
239 - 169 B.C.

Why stand ye here all the day idle?
— Matthew 20:6

September 3

TOIL IS SWEET

Doing all you can for yourself is very suggestive of thought and toil, encouraged by faith and supported by perseverance. God wills us well in life; but if God's will is done, we must perform our work.

The state of comfort and ease is not as pleasant as some think. It is wrought with dissappointments: muscles weaken, eyes drop and hearts lose their zest. No interest! No challenge! No stimulation!

What the overly comfortable need is another mountain to climb, at least a hill, for down-hill living lowers man.

Our toil is sweet with thankfulness,
Our burden is our boon;
The curse of earth's gray morning is
The blessing of its noon.

—*John Greenleaf Whittier*
1807 - 1892

Fulfill your works, your daily tasks . . .
—Exodus 5:13

September 4

STRIVING BRINGS THRIVING

A lazy person and a fruitless tree go together — the tree makes the shade, the indolent sits in it. Neither produces.

Hard work plants the seed and reaps the fruits. Laziness harvests nothing, nothing but woes.

Industry clears the mind, strengthens the body, guards the soul and fills the purse. It encourages honesty and peacefulness, for there is less temptation to steal and cause trouble. It gives a satisfaction and contentment that idleness can never know. And if I had to choose one or the other, I had rather have industry without genius than genius without industry.

> *Good striving*
> *Brings thriving*
> *Better a dog who works*
> *Than a lion who shirks.*
>
> *—From the Persian*

Slothfulness casteth into a deep sleep; and an idle soul shall suffer hunger.
—Proverbs 19:15

September 5

SUCCESS IS DILIGENT

Whole-heartedness and success.
Diligence and victory.
Indolence and failure.
Unsteadfastness and defeat.

Here we have four sets of siamese twins, and the whole world knows they belong together as we have linked them.

But indolence and success, unsteadfastness and victory, are not even fourth cousins; so there is no way to relate them. For only like kind are like kin.

The Success Family is very distinctive. It has no lazy or wavery children.

Diligence is the mother of good fortune.
—*Miguel de Cervantes*
1547 - 1616

The thoughts of the diligent tend only to plenteousness.—Proverbs 21:5

September 6

THE RIGHT OF WAGES

Labor was appointed at the creation, but so was its remuneration. "In the sweat of thy face shalt thou eat bread." Labor and sustenance go together. The right to enjoy the fruits of his work is one of man's earliest rights, stretching all the way back to the dawn of time. It is a God-given due.

If we deny a person his just wages, we deny him the freedom to live. You take his life, if you take that which sustains life. Toil should not go unrewarded! Even the working animal is entitled to eat.

You take my house, when you do take the prop
That doth sustain my house; you take my life,
When you do take the means whereby I live.

—*William Shakespeare*
1564 - 1616

Thou shalt not muzzle the mouth of the ox that treadeth out the corn.—I Corinthians 9:9

HARDER TO FAIL

It is hard for a person to be what he ought to be, but it is much harder not to be.

It is not easy to earn a living, but it is a lot easier than starving or begging or stealing.

The price of morality is high, but the price of immorality is higher.

It is tiresome to bear your burdens, but to refuse is not restful.

There are bitter circumstances which try a person's politeness, but rudeness sweetens nothing, only adds bitter to bitters.

It is hard to do anything meritorious, but it is a thousand times harder to fail.

And though hard be the task,
"Keep a stiff upper lip."

—*Phoebe Cary*
1824 - 1871

Thou hast showed thy people hard things.—Psalms 60:3

BE LOYAL

Loyalty gives unmixed support. It is true in word, faithful in deed, devoid of hypocrisy, free from betrayal; and when Judases sell out, it can't be bought.

It is so appreciated that the world treasures one ounce of it more than a pound of cleverness.

Therefore, whatever relationships you have that demand loyalty, be true to them. If you hire out to a man, work for him. If he supplies your bread and butter, you supply devotion and dedication. As long as you work at a place, work for it. Give an undivided service or none. If you can't be loyal, leave.

> *It is not book learning young men need, nor instruction about this and that, but a stiffening of the vertebrae which will cause them to be loyal to a trust.*
>
> *—Elbert Hubbard*

And ye know that with all my power I have served your father.—Genesis 31:6

DIFFICULTIES DEVELOP US

Don't fret because of difficulties. They show what men are made of.

When obstacles are piled high and you climb over them, you have ascended higher than you would have without them. They are nature's way of developing strength. Just sitting in an easy chair and eating off a silver platter is no way to develop a man's best.

It takes strenuous effort to climb a mountain, but half the joy of looking from the peak is due to the difficult climb. And traveling a pathway of thorns teaches doggedness, caution, sympathy, and consequently the goal is more appreciated.

> *No traveler e'er reached that blest abode*
> *Who found not thorns and briers in his road.*
>
> —*William Cowper*
> 1731 - 1800

How that in a great trial of affliction, the abundance of their joy and their deep poverty abounded unto the riches of their liberality.—II Corinthians 8:2

AFFINITY TELLS

Show me the company a man keeps and the books he reads, and I shall tell you what kind of a man he is. For where there is attraction, there is likeness. Some literature appeals. And some people are his kind.

Man seeks to please himself. If a book doesn't satisfy, then he's not going to read it. Neither will he maintain associations that are unenjoyable. He gravitates toward the people of which he is a part; and he goes out from certain others, because he is not of them. Like minds effect togetherness; unlike ones affect their feet — in opposite directions.

Show me his friends and I the man shall know;
This wiser turn a larger wisdom lends:
Show me the books he loves and I shall know
The man far better than through mortal friends

—*Silas Weir Mitchell*

They went out from us, but they were not of us; for if they had been of us, they would no doubt have continued with us.— I John 2:19

September 11

THINK AND BE FREE

Man is so constituted that when he is struck with a thought, it ought not to be an accident. Man's distinction is his ability to think for himself.

When brains don't think — though educated — man is caged within the confines of what another gives him, good or bad. Little cages are for thinkless parrots, but the wide universe is for thinking man. The heavens and the earth stand ajar for him who thinks; if you don't, you must remain in your cage and parrot cute little phrases for those who feed you.

> *Thought takes man out of servitude, into freedom.*
>
> —*Henry Wadsworth Longfellow*
> 1807 - 1882

...one would think the deep to be hoary.
— Job 41:32

FOR LIFE TO BE REWARDING

For life to be the fullest, sweetest and most rewarding:

— Do more than move; improve.
— Do more than get; give.
— Do more than regret; repent.
— Do more than look; see.
— Do more than sympathize; help.
— Do more than attend church; worship.
— Do more than have children; rear them.
— Do more than build a house; make a home.
— Do more than breathe; live.
— Do more than live; love.

We live in deeds, not years; in thoughts, not breaths,
In feelings, not in figures on a dial.
We should count time by heart-throbs.
*   He most lives*
Who thinks most. feels the noblest, acts the best.
*   —Philip James Bailey*

We spend our years as a tale that is told.
— Psalms 90:9

CHANGE THE CAUSE

Every consequence has a reason. Hence, if you would improve your lot, work on the causes. This is better than whining over effects. Shaping causes is a prerogative of man; and as he does, he changes himself and the world.

This is what life is all about — causes and effects. Man plants a crop and reaps a harvest, digs a well and has water, throws up a dam and makes a lake, slants his mind and so becomes the man.

This principle distinguishes the corrector from the complainer, the gainer from the grumbler, the haves from the have-nots.

> *Don't curse the darkness — light a candle.*
> *—Chinese Proverb*

Is there not a cause?   — I Samuel 17:29

A REFINEMENT CALLED COURTESY

Courtesy pays. To the receiver it distributes amiability. To the exhibitor it adds both personality and fortune. It makes one a gentleman — gentle man — who does things gently and lovingly.

It opens hearts which, in turn, opens purses. A wealthy merchant stated that he owed his fortune to Joseph, of the Old Testament, from whom he had gleaned his business policy: "The customer is right, though he is wrong." He found it more profitable in the end to exhibit a special courtesy to the purchaser than to contend for his own rights. Courtesy is truly a coin that passes at par in any nation.

We must be courteous to a man as we are to a picture, which we are willing to give the advantage of a good light.

—*Ralph Waldo Emerson*
1803 - 1882

And he comforted them and spoke kindly unto them.—Genesis 50:21

SUCCESS DEMANDS HONESTY

The way of success is not wide enough for crooked dealings. It shouts to the wayfarer, "If you would travel me, leave behind deceit, dishonesty and skullduggery." It is a road for only the upright. Though it may appear that the dishonest can traverse it, sooner or later they hit the bumps and land in the ditch.

The honest journeyer has the advantage of being able to travel day or night, but the crook has a feeling of false security in only night driving.

The road to success looks narrow, but it is broad enough to handle the traffic. There is room on it for the hard driving, efficient, honest man.

Honest labor bears a lovely face.

—Thomas Dekker
1572 - 1632

The integrity of the upright shall guide them.—Proverbs 11:3

MAKINGS OF A MAN

That man is a man! Not by birth, but life. Not for his stature, but for his heart. Gold doesn't seduce his hands; honor doesn't turn his head; dishonor doesn't turn his feet; fear doesn't curl his backbone; disappointment doesn't crush his heart.

He's a man day and night, in the light and in the dark, in prosperity and in adversity.

He has quality, and that — not pounds, not inches, not color — makes a man.

His grandeur is in his ideals, his beliefs, his practices — and there the world should apply the gauges. For the great hope of our society is in having more people like him.

His life was gentle, and the elements
So mix'd in him that Nature might stand up
And say to all the world, "This was a man!"

—William Shakespeare
1564 - 1616

Be thou strong therefore, and show thyself a man.—I Kings 2:2

AGE CAN BE RIPENED YOUTH

The only true gauge of life is action — not pounds and inches. And the only true measurement of age is attitude — not birthdays.

This is why some people become old at thirty, while others remain young at eighty. Let's not confuse age with anniversaries. Though you have seen fourscore years, you are just ripening youth if you:

— Love life.
— Enjoy living.
— Are hopeful.
— Seek new thoughts for stimulation.
— Find new ways to do old things.
— Raise new ladders to climb.
— Enter new fields to gather.

Furthermore, there is a chance for you.

For what is age but youth's full bloom,
A riper, more transcendent youth?
A weight of gold is never old.

—Anonymous

And now, lo, I am this day fourscore and five years old. As yet I am as strong this day as I was in the day that Moses sent me—Joshua 14:10, 11

BE LOYAL TO SELF

Self-loyalty! An ingredient of every worthwhile: character, goodness, honor, accomplishment!

We can survive the betrayal of supposed friends, but not self. In tragic life, the disloyalty that destroys is within. There the plot thickens. There the villain resides. The Judases without are not half as deadly as the Judas within. Others can let us down and we can still come out on top, but not if we let ourselves down. It is hard to recover from self-inflicted blows.

Be true to self and you can look friend and foe in the eye; betray yourself and your countenance falls.

In tragic life, God wot,
No villain need be! Passions spin the plot:
We are betrayed by what is false within.

—George Meredith

Create in me a clean heart, O God; and renew a right spirit within me.—Psalms 51:10

NO IMITATOR

You are worth more being you than trying to be somebody else. It saves you from having to act — no theatrical performances. Neither do you have to suffer the mockery life heaps on the pretender. Furthermore, your singleness of personality — not multiple selves — brings an internal peace never known by the imitator.

Being you is more impressive; no make-believer is believed very long. It gives more energy; acting is hard work. It affords habitual and spontaneous reactions, because there is no delay in trying to read another's lines. You can be independent; for trying to be another is like being the tail on another dog — he wags you.

Posterity weaves no garlands for imitators.

—Johann Christoph Friedrich von Schiller
1759 - 1805

Why feignest thou thyself to be another?
—I Kings 14:6

September 20

LIBRARY IN ONE VOLUME

A knowledge of the Bible is essential to scholarship in many fields. The libraries of the world are to a large extent commentaries and elaborations on the principles laid down in the Bible. It is truly a library within itself.

The man who knows it is a scholar and if he follows it, a gentleman. "Of making many books, there is no end," but none takes the place of the Book. It is as inexhaustible as dipping up the ocean with a spoon. It challenges the best minds, and though they read it a thousand times, something new is gleaned from every reading.

I thoroughly believe in university education for both men and women, but I believe a knowledge of the Bible without a college course is more valuable than a college course without the Bible.

—*William Lyon Phelps*
(Called the most beloved professor of America — of Yale University.)

Thy word is a lamp unto my feet, and a light unto my path.—Psalms 119:105

NEVER FIGHT FOR THE LAST WORD

Having the last say does not say you are first. Any person with the biggest muscle and the least brain can have the last say. Greatness is not in the last word, but in the wisest word. And the wisest word is often no word — silence. We are seldom hurt by what we don't say.

When peace is threatened, it is better to draw on your self-control and say nothing than to draw on your vocabulary and say something that adds nothing. A good talker knows when. Who keeps his tongue, keeps peace — and friends.

> *The last word is the most dangerous of infernal machines, and the husband and wife should no more fight to get it than they would struggle for the possession of a lighted bombshell.*
>
> *—Douglas Jerrold*
> 1803 - 1857

A fool's lips enter into contention, and his mouth calleth for strokes.—Proverbs 18:6

FAME NEEDS A CRISIS

We never recognize those worthy of fame until the test comes. The greatness is there all time, but it takes the testing to discover it. There had to be a historic cause before there could rise a historic George Washington.

Think of the many greats whose names could be handed down to the ages, but who, because of a lack of testing, shall sleep in barely known graves that shall soon lose their little distinction. Untried, they walk along with the mediocre, hardly distinguishable. It's the crisis which distinguishes men, allowing one to surpass another.

Their noonday never knows
What names immortal are;
'Tis night alone that shows
How star surpasseth star.

—John Bannister Tabb

And have made thee a great name, like unto the name of the great men that are in the earth.—II Samuel 7:9

INGRATITUDE COOLS FRIENDSHIP

Perhaps there is nothing that cools friendships quicker than ingratitude. It is a member of a wicked family: pride, selfishness, unhappiness, baseness. The proud is not thankful — too hard for him to bow; neither is the selfish — feels he has everything coming; nor is the malcontent — nothing thrills him; nor is the base — his character is too weak to be thankful.

About all the ingrate is good at is biting the hand that hands him favors — a hand-biter.

Thanks! how inadequately it expresses our feelings. But until we come up with a better word, learn to say it: *Thanks! Thanks! Thanks!*

> *Blow, blow, thou winter wind!*
> *Thou art not so unkind*
> *As man's ingratitude.*
>
> —*William Shakespears*
> 1564 - 1616

For men shall be lovers of their own selves, covetous, boasters, proud, blasphemers, disobedient to parents, unthankful, unholy.—II Timothy 3:2

LOOK BENEATH APPEARANCES

It's not the fashion that's on a man that counts most. You can hang a tie on anything. A dirty life can bathe and carry an odor of cologne. A scoundrel can dress in a silken suit. A fake can sit behind the wheel of a late model car, if! if! you will carry the notes.

Such goods are good, provided there is a real man to go with them. For it is within a man that his actual worth exists, and from there all genuine progress must come. The source of bona fide living is down deep in a man — not on the surface.

> *Do not conceive that fine clothes make fine men, anymore than fine feathers make fine birds.*
>
> *—George Washington*
> 1732 - 1799

> Do ye look on things after the outward appearance?—II Corinthians 10:7

September 25

WHEN FOLLOWING OTHERS

Our society calls for some to lead and others to follow. It takes the combination of the two — leadership and followship — for we cannot have one without the other. There is nothing wrong with following provided you are led rather than misled. Whether you lead or follow, be sure to keep your eyes open. Don't be led around with a blind bridle. Probably one of the most famous of all epitaphs is one which reads:

Stranger, stop as you pass by;
As you are now, so once was I.
As I am now, you soon will be;
And so prepare to follow me.

Someone who read this sentiment on the tombstone evidently gave it serious consideration and then wisely added these two lines:

To follow you I'm not content,
Until I know which way you went.

And if the blind lead the blind, both shall fall into the ditch.—Matthew 15:14

GOLD IN THOSE MISFORTUNES

Misfortune has its fringe benefits, even though we seldom recognize them at the time. Much of our soul-searching, resolutions, alterations, trust, sympathy and even prosperity have come to us through what appeared to be reverses.

The story has been told of a poor miller whose mill and home were washed away by a flood. Standing on the site, feeling helpless and hopeless, he saw something shining in the bank. It was gold. That which impoverished him made him rich. And so it may be with us. Our adversity may become our gold.

> *Fire is the test of gold; adversity, of strong men.*
> —*Lucius Annaeus Seneca*
> 8 B.C. - A.D. 65

When he hath tried me, I shall come forth as gold.—Job 23:10

TAUGHT BY THE YEARS

The years should teach us that to "rush in where angels dare to tread" is the surest way to get knocked down and dragged out; that fairness requires hearing both sides; that we had to grow before we were prepared to accept some opportunities we wanted too early; that if we cut out the fear of things that never happen, we will reduce our troubles ninety percent; that brains in the head and love in the heart will solve most problems; that suckerbait no longer looks appetizing, for we have had our fill; that we still have a chance.

> *The years teach much which the days never know.*
> —*Ralph Waldo Emerson*
> 1803 - 1882

Days should speak, and multitude of years should teach wisdom.—Job 32:7

WAGE YOUR BEST

Do your best. Not even the elements can do better. For a raindrop can give only so much moisture; a star only so much light; and a human being only so much productivity. Nature functions to its full capacity, and so should man.

If it's right to live up to your potentiality, then it's wrong to drop below it: so wrong that nature has decreed that you live up to your talents and opportunities or lose them.

After you have done your best, there is only one other thing you can do — trust God for the rest. Angels can do no more.

> *...learn to do thy part*
> *And leave the rest to Heaven.*
>
> *—John Henry Newman*
> 1801 - 1890

Zaccheus . . . sought to see Jesus who he was; and could not for the press, because he was little of stature. And he ran before, and climbed up into a sycamore tree to see him; for he was to pass that way.—Luke 19:2-4

ONLY THE FEARLESS ARE FREE

You must conquer fear or be a slave. No slave chains or iron bars are as restricting as fear. It is ridiculous for one to talk about "America, the land of the free and the brave" while he wears the ball and chain of fear.

No person is free who is afraid to try lest he fail; or who fears to break with tradition; or who is scared to stand for right when in its ranks there are only the few; or who is frightened to speak the truth when the masses hold to error; or who is too chicken-hearted to be his own master.

They are slaves who fear to speak
For the fallen and the weak;
They are slaves who will not choose
Hatred, scoffing, and abuse,
Rather than in silence shrink
From the truth they needs must think;
They are slaves who dare not be
In the right with two or three.

—James Russell Lowell
1819 - 1891

I was afraid . . . and I hid myself.—Genesis 3:10

MAKING LIFE COUNT

Life is too short and precious to waste. It is wrought with too many possibilities for accomplishment and happiness to fling it away. Don't squander yourself on the frustrating dissipations of cynicism, hate, envy, retaliation, faultfinding, pessimism, gossip, idleness, doubt, debauchery.

Make life count! Give yourself to every day's dawn of renewed life, found in the flourishing qualities like love, forgiveness, tolerance, optimism, temperance, industry, faith, righteousness. Let these be your moments, and time shall pass to the conservation of your life and to the making of a new calendar, not measured in clock ticks but heart beats.

Life is too short to waste
In critic peep or cynic bark,
Quarrel or reprimand.
'Twill soon be dark;
Up! mind thine own aim, and
God speed the mark!

—*Ralph Waldo Emerson*
1803 - 1882

For we must needs die, and are as water spilt on the ground, which cannot be gathered up again.—II Samuel 14:14

HAVE HOPE

Nothing brightens the day more than anticipation. It quickens the heart and sets the soul aflame. It gives courage "to bear those ills we have." Anticipation guards every day against dullness and despair. It bridges our adversities.

Man is a creature of hope; our world is a place of hope; and the person without it is a misfit. There are no hopeless situations; only hopeless people make situations appear hopeless. Hope never says, "Let's quit." Though the night is dark, hope knows that every day has a morning. Hope gives an easier today, for it anticipates a better tomorrow.

Have hope. Though clouds environ now,
And gladness hides her face in scorn,
Put thou the shadow from thy brow —
No night but hath its morn.

—Johann Christoph Friedrich von Schiller
1750 - 1805

And thou shalt be secure because there is hope.—Job 11:18

HANDLING PROBLEMS

Every hour brings its own troubles. Hence, how do we handle the little worries, disappointments and tensions of everyday living?

In the first place, be realistic enough to know that they will come. A willing acceptance of them makes for calmness and rationalism as you face them.

Secondly, you can break each blow by bending with it. By stooping with sweet condescension you lessen the impact. Bending when you can is preferable to breaking, and submitting where there is no violation of principle is better than being crushed. The merit is in solving the problem — not in rebelling at it.

> *Though trouble-tossed and torture-torn*
> *The kingliest kings are crowned with thorn.*
>
> *—Gerald Massey*

Hear counsel, and receive instruction, that thou mayest be wise in thy latter end.—Proverbs 19:20

BE NOT DECEIVED

Investigate! Watch the deceivers and defrauders, fleecers and flimflammers, hoaxers and hypocrites. Look before you leap. That soft landing prepared by the humbugs may be jerked out from under you.

The scoundrels are professors of virtue, but not possessors of it. They are artists in deception, actors who make quackery sound good. They count on a man's gullibility, his disinclination to investigate.

They carry a bag of tricks: They play on honesty when they are dishonest; they appeal to truth when they are liars; they say they love you when they love themselves; and they quote Scripture when they don't believe it.

The devil can cite Scripture for his purpose.

—William Shakespeare
1564 - 1616

And saith unto him, If thou be the Son of God, cast thyself down: for it is written, He shall give his angels charge concerning thee . . .—Matthew 4:6

PASSING OVER INSULTS

Pass it by! The slur, the slight, the catty remark, we suffer from others. A refusal to forget it would keep us in war always. Our circle of friends would diminish; our blood pressure would go up; and our efficiency would go down. After all, most of us need just about as much tolerance from others as we need to extend to them.

We should never be insulted by any moral and well-bred person, for he would not intentionally do it. Neither should we be affronted by any others, for they are not worthy to hurt us.

A moral, sensible, and well-bred man
Will not affront me, and no other can.

—*William Cowper*
1731 - 1800

The discretion of a man deferreth his anger; and it is his glory to pass over a transgression.—Proverbs 19:11

MATTER OF MASTERY

There is no way to excel without exerting a greater power than the opposing forces wield. That is what triumph is — overcoming rather than being overcome. Success or failure is simply a matter of mastery — we conquer or get conquered.

Our world is one of struggles. Man becomes educated by outsmarting ignorance; courteous by prevailing over rudeness; industrious by winning over slothfulness; superior by outdoing inferiority; and good by overcoming evil.

In all these tests man first struggles within himself where he first wins or loses. Take heart — and win!

> *Not in the clamor of the crowded street,*
> *Not in the shouts and plaudits of the throne,*
> *But in ourselves are triumph and defeat.*
>
> *—Henry Wadsworth Longfellow*
> 1807 - 1882

For of whom a man is overcome, of the same is he brought in bondage.—II Peter 2:19

CONQUERED FAULTS

Unless your virtues have come through self-determination and rigorous development, you cannot fancy yourself a victor. There is no test of goodness in being polite toward the affable, patient toward those you fear or whose favor you court, or charitable toward those you love.

But there is merit — real merit — in conquering your faults. Take one — just one: gossip, slothfulness, sulkiness, uncharitableness, revenge, pride, envy, swearing or impulsiveness, and attack it bravely. It will take weeks — not to completely eradicate it — just to prevent its dominating you. With that one subdued, then tackle another. It takes effort, but it gives satisfaction.

We rise by the things that are under feet;
By what we have mastered of good and gain,
By the pride deposed and the passion slain,
And the vanquished ills that we hourly meet.

—Josiah Gilbert Holland
1819 - 1881

... put off the old man ... put on the new man . . .—Colossians 3:9, 10

BLESSED BY BOOKS

Books! What treasures! Old books make us heirs of the distant past. New books put us in closer touch with our contemporaries. Old or new, books convert the reader's mind into a throne where knowledge reigns. And where knowledge rules, poverty is overcome, sorrow is healed, misery is cured, and oppression is lifted from bent and galled backs.

There is some hope for a person who reads good books, especially the kind that make you think. Get in the habit of carrying a volume with you. Have a nightcap book that climaxes the day with enrichment before you sleep.

How many a man has dated a new era in his life from the reading of a book.

—*Henry David Thoreau*
1817 - 1862

The cloak that I left at Troas with Carpus, when thou comest, bring with thee, and the books, but especially the parchments.—II Timothy 4:13

LITTLE THINGS

Cherish the little things. They are often the most precious. Little words are the sweetest to the ear: God, church, Bible, faith, hope, love, mother, home, child.

Most of life revolves around the *littles* — little words and little deeds — but they are so necessary that they are enormous. A little cup of cold water, given a thirsty traveler, is big in the sight of heaven. Little songs enrapture the fullest. Little hearts arouse to the widest-eyed excitement. Simple joys last the longest.

Big people are made up of many *littles*.

It's the little things which keep the world shining — little beams by day and little twinkles by night.

Man wants but little, nor that little long.

—*Edward Young*
1683 - 1765

. . . a little balm, and a little honey, spices and myrrh, nuts and almonds.—
Genesis 43:11

EASIER MADE THAN PAID

"Easy Payments" are not always easy. Slavish liabilities will deny you today, for you will have to give it in worry and sweat and blood to others.

If you can't refrain from buying the things you can't afford, your obligations will pile up like mountains; and then life will be an uphill pull for you — too much to lug and too high to climb.

There are better ways than defaulting in debts to have the world beating a path to your door.

There was a time when delinquent debtors were stoned; today they are blackballed.

Debt and misery live on the same road.

—Russian Proverb

Be not thou one of them that strike hands, or of them that are sureties for debts. If thou hast nothing to pay, why should he take away thy bed from under thee?—Proverbs 22:26, 27

DEED SPEAKS LOUDER THAN CREED

Our deeds say more than our words. What we do is what we are. What we say may be only what we want others to think we are. Man becomes the story of his own deeds; they make the man, and they tell what kind of man they have made. You might mistake a man's creed, but not his deed.

A busy tongue with still hands is inappropriate. Remember — nobody appreciates the sound of the clock unless there is movement of the hands. Keep ticking, but keep moving!

Well done is better than well said.

—Benjamin Franklin
1706 - 1790

A certain man had two sons; and he came to the first, and said, Son, go work today in my vineyard. He answered and said, I will not; but afterward he repented, and went. And he came to the second, and said likewise. And he answered and said, I go, sir; and went not. Whether of them twain did the will of his father?—Matthew 21:28-31

WITHOUT HYPOCRISY

It is innocent and proper for children to wear false faces on Halloween, but not for adults all during the year. Hypocrisy is loose double-dealings, and when they strike together, the noise is so deafening you cannot hear the person speak; for what he is drowns out what he says.

Though one becomes blind to himself, others can see through him.

If man allows himself to deal in duplicity, it will grow and grow until he becomes a spectacle of deceit, completely devoid of reason. He becomes as ridiculous as the man Lincoln spoke of "who murdered his parents and pleaded for mercy on the grounds that he was an orphan."

You may fool all the people some of the time; you can even fool some of the people all of the time; but you can't fool all of the people all the time.
—*Abraham Lincoln*
1809 - 1865

But the wisdom that is from above is ... without hypocrisy.—James 3:17

A NEW WORLD

You can discover a new world. You can! And if you would:

— Desire a world better than the one you now occupy.
— Have faith that it exists, that it is not fantasy. It is as real as one wishes to make it. Believe you can find it, for you can.
— Launch your ship. Lift the anchor. Set the sails, and no matter which way the wind blows, you shall be carried on your way.
— Persevere. There are no happy lands over yonder for the fainthearted. Have the spirit of Columbus who sailed on and on.

> *They sailed. They sailed. Then spoke the mate:*
> *"This mad sea shows its teeth to-night.*
> *He curls his lip, he lies in wait,*
> *With lifted teeth, as if to bite!*
> *Brave Admiral, say but one good word.*
> *What shall we do when hope is gone?"*
> *The words leapt as a leaping sword,*
> *"Sail on! sail on! sail on! and on!"*
>
> *—Joaquin Miller*

He raiseth up the poor out of the dust, and lifteth up the beggar from the dunghill, to set them among princes, and to make them inherit the throne of glory: for the pillars of the earth are the Lord's, and he hath set the world upon them.—I Samuel 2:8

HUMILITY

The truly great person never feels any worthy task is too low for him.

When James Madison completed his eight years as President, he retired to his Virginia plantation and filled the office of justice of the peace. No wonder he had climbed up, for he knew how to climb down. He didn't have to appear to be great, for he was; and no office could make him less. His meekness was not weakness. His humility was not humiliation.

The size of the job is not half as honorable as the size of the man who fills it.

> *I believe the first test of a truly great man is his humility.*
>
> —*John Ruskin*
> 1819 - 1900

By humility and the fear of the Lord are riches, and honor, and life.—Proverbs 22:4

ONE BLOOD

After all is said, there is but one race — man — and to it every man belongs. All have the same lineage, a common ancestry. Thus man — not kinds — is the master race with dominion over every other creature.

And in the gain or loss of one man the whole race is lifted or lowered. If there is hope for humanity, we must find it in and for all. Being of the same ancestry, blood should be stronger than prejudice; it is, and in time shall prevail. In this, the rationalism of a common blood, is one hope for civilization.

We be of one blood, ye and I.

—*Rudyard Kipling*

And hath made of one blood all nations of men for to dwell on all the face of the earth.
—Acts 17:26

PULL AHEAD BY THINKING

In our fast-moving world, take time to step aside and think. Later you can pass up the ones who didn't. Unless there is straight thinking, there can be no straight traveling. To avoid leaving zigzag and reverse tracks on the sands of time, think! For as you think, you travel. Thinking can figure out the shortcuts. This is why some people are always ahead — they outthink the rest of them.

Think! For no person can outdistance his thoughts. You are today where your thoughts were yesterday, and you shall be tomorrow where your thoughts are today.

The more you think, the more time you have.
                                    —*Henry Ford*

I thought on my ways, and turned my feet unto thy testimonies.—Psalms 119:59

PRAISE HELPS

Pass on the praise! For all are mortal enough to love it. Its helpfulness, however, is found in its being deserved — that separates it from flattery. And everybody has something worthy of praise. See it. Speak it.

An appreciative word may create a new resolve. Praising something you like in a person, any person, even the man in the gutter, invigorates him. If a person is good at a thing, tell him he is; if he gets better, tell him again; if he becomes best, tell him again. It will help him — and you — to tell him.

> *Try praising your wife, even if it does frighten her at first.*
> —*Billy Sunday*

Her children arise up, and call her blessed; her husband also, and he praiseth her.
—Proverbs 31:28

KEEP YOUR RELIGION WOUND UP

Wind up your religion by going to church. Anybody can run down.

As the big clock was striking the hour very slowly, grandpa remarked: "Sounds like the striking part of it is nearly run down."

An hour later while he was reading the Sunday paper, grandmother came in and inquired if he were going to church.

He slowly answered, "Oh, I — I guess so."

She replied, "Sounds as if the church side of you is nearly run down! Is it?"

Grandpa blushed and said, "Maybe it is, but we'll wind it up again."

Your religion, like your clock, has to be wound up, if it ticks.

CH??CH
What is missing?

—*Anonymous*

Not forsaking the assembling of ourselves together, as the manner of some is.
— Hebrews 10:25

WILL POWER

Hold the reins! Don't be a runaway.

An old stage-driver, after thirty years of experience, commented that he had never hurt a passenger nor a horse, simply because he always kept a firm grip on the reins. "The whole secret is in not letting the horses get the start," he said.

This is good philosophy for controlling self: Hold the reins; hold yourself back from bad habits. You never become a runaway in a thing you never start. No one is stronger than his will. Unless you have will power, you have no power. For where there is no will, there is no way.

> *The truest wisdom, in general, is a resolute determination.*
> —*Napoleon Bonaparte*
> 1769 - 1821

But I keep under my body, and bring it into subjection.—I Corinthians 9:27

THINK BEFORE SPEAKING

It is easier to say what you think than to think what you say. There is wisdom in holding back the full utterance of your mind for the more opportune time. Knowing what to say and when to say it will put you among the great! and the peaceful! and the happy!

When you have a thing to say, say it, but not until you know how and when. Be sure it does good. An excellent rule to follow is to say only what you would be willing to have on your lips if they should never speak again.

He that would live in peace and ease must not speak all he knows nor judge all he sees.

—Benjamin Franklin
1706 - 1790

A fool uttereth all his mind; but a wise man keepeth it in till afterward.—Proverbs 29:11

MY ANCESTORS' OFFSPRING

It is desirable to have renowned blood, but the praise belongs to our forefathers, not us. The only glory I can claim is what I earn. I am just a limb on a genealogical tree; and if it bears fruit today, it has to bear it through *me*.

The plain fact is — every family line has the good and the bad, the king and the slave. Who my great-great-grandfather was is not half as important as what his great-great-grandson will be. Thus, it is fitting that I give less thought to my ancestors and more attention to this offspring of theirs.

Who serves his country well has no need of ancestors.
—*Voltaire*
1694 - 1778

And Solomon did evil in the sight of the Lord, and went not fully after the Lord, as did David his father.—I Kings 11:6

COURTESY OPENS HEARTS

Hearts are apt to open for you, if you use the priceless key of courtesy. It fits almost every locked heart.

Like responds to like. Use a courteous approach and you will get a courteous reception — with few exceptions.

You don't crash hearts — they are opened from within. And they open better if the hinges are lubricated with the oil of graciousness. It prevents friction. It is a smoothness that finds easygoingness everywhere.

Politeness is so necessary to better relations that it should be a part of every person's religion. It is religion! For it is an expression of the Golden Rule.

By being polite and friendly, you can make people pliable and obliging.

—Arthur Schopenhauer
1788 - 1860

The words of a wise man's mouth are gracious.—Ecclesiastes 10:12

THE BEAUTY THAT WINS

Good looks are at a premium everywhere. Appearance is an asset to any creature, but not the ultimate in values. A person with good looks and fine physique has an advantage, but not enough to win without a winsome personality, charming manners, sterling character and a sharp mind.

Comeliness commends, but never wins — in the long run; for in the home stretch it's the inward beauty that years can't fade, that comes in ahead. There are born beauties, but no born winners. Handsomeness never makes the man — just makes him more marketable.

Beauty without grace is the hook without the bait.
            —*Ralph Waldo Emerson*
            1803 - 1882

But the Lord said unto Samuel, Look not on his countenance, or on the height of his stature; because I have refused him.
— I Samuel 16:7

RICHEST RICHES

It was the famous Patrick Henry who wrote in his will: "This is all the inheritance I can give to my dear family. The religion of Christ will give them one which will make them rich indeed."

Man's most precious riches are in the heart, not the purse. If the heart is filled with faith, hope, love, self-respect, peace and good will, that person is rich. The richest rich! Because those means supply the greatest need!

Therefore, while you are laying up some valuables for the physical man, neglect not to put a few in the heart. They count most!

> *It is bad to have an empty purse,*
> *But an empty heart is a whole lot worse.*
>
> —*Nixon Waterman*

There is that maketh himself rich yet hath nothing: there is that maketh himself poor, yet hath great riches.—Proverbs 13:7

DON'T IMAGINE TROUBLE

Unless a person watches his imagination, he is sure to have more troubles than he can handle. He already has enough without entertaining some in fantasy.

Horrible imaginations give you shadowy dangers and unreal burdens, but they scare and tire as much as if they were genuine.

It is more practical to be realistic, to see things as they are, no better or worse; for some people have troubles and don't know it, while others don't have troubles and know they do.

It was Mark Twain who said, "I am an old man and have known a great many troubles, but most of them never happened."

> *Though life is made up of mere bubbles*
> *'Tis better than many aver,*
> *For while we've a whole lot of troubles*
> *The most of them never occur.*
>
> *—Nixon Waterman*

Behold, I know your thoughts, and the devices which ye wrongfully imagine against me.
— Job 21:27

PICK THE TIME TO ACT

Discretion is the better part of wisdom — and of valor. Any fool can speak or act at the wrong time. No matter how good a word or deed may be, there are times when it is inappropriate. Even the fox is known for his superior prudence; he picks his time to strike.

The best of talents will fail, if the use of them is not properly timed. After all, even judgment is needed to fly a kite — not every day is a likely time. To know when to act is a whole education wrapped up in one word — discretion.

I had a thing to say,
But I will fit with some better time.

—William Shakespeare
1564 - 1616

To every thing there is a season, and a time to every purpose under the heaven...
a time to keep silence, and a time to speak.
— Ecclesiastes 3:1-7

HALF AND HALF RELIGION

Halfway religion is no religion, for religion plus a certain feeling against religion equals nothing. The calling to serve God will not tolerate a lukewarm state that is neither hot nor cold, a little for and a little against. It won't do any good to reluctantly bow in prayer on mocking knees and lisp with a forked tongue halfhearted words.

Contrariwise, giving God undivided devotion is the most sustaining experience in all the world. It will warm and enlarge your heart for God and man, and give you strength to stand up to any eventuality, come what may.

Thou hast made us for Thyself, O Lord;
and our heart is restless until it rests in Thee.

—St. Augustine
354 - 430

So then because thou art lukewarm, and neither cold nor hot, I will spew thee out of my mouth. — Revelation 3:16

THANKS

"I thank you" are three very important words. Learn to speak them. Naturally. Sincerely. No person deserves more than he is thankful for. And the size of one's gratitude is not dependent upon the size of the object or favor received, but rather upon the size of the heart.

Gratefulness is a basic support which keeps life from sagging. It is a necessary quality of greatness and nobility. It is a prerequisite of happiness, for no soul's joy can be deeper than his thankfulness. Furthermore, it is an excellent way to return a gift — just say, "I thank you," for this is a payment to the giver.

> *I can no other answer make but thanks,*
> *and thanks, and ever thanks.*

—*William Shakespeare*
1564 - 1616

. . . be ye thankful.—Colossians 3:15

FACE TO FACE

There are many advantages in coming face to face with the person from whom you have become estranged. It creates a warmth that distance will not generate. It permits a smile to speak a rhetoric that cannot be worded. Personal bigness is tested. Tolerance becomes more tolerant, understanding more understandable.

The little differences begin to shrink, because you are in the presence of something bigger, the person himself. It grants each an eyesight of the other, no horns, no pitchforks. It lets you see your grievance in his face, and there you have a better chance to behold his motive and not his act.

Face to face brings you to the intent,
And to how he erred in what he meant.

—Anonymous

Come, let us look one another in the face.
— II Kings 14:8

NEVER AGGRAVATE STRIFE

Let us learn from a fable, an intentional travesty of human folly:

A man encountered a strange varment on a narrow road. He could have passed it by, but he didn't. He struck it with a club and continued his journey. Soon afterwards the obnoxious creature overtook him, now three times as big and ferocious as before. Not one to be outdone, the man struck it hard, again and again; but the more he clubbed the animal, the more he aggravated it and the bigger it grew.

The name of the monster is Strife. Its size and ferocity depend much upon your attitude toward it.

We call ourselves "civilized," but the strife about us proves our error.

—J. Wesley Dickson

Surely the churning of milk bringeth forth butter, and the wringing of the nose bringeth forth blood: so the forcing of wrath bringeth forth strife.—Proverbs 30:33

MORE PEACE IN A BIG HEART

Peace of heart depends on the heart — what you are, not where you are. There is no need to look for it beyond the mountains nor over the seas. Neither will you find it in what you possess, but rather in what possesses you.

If you find peace, it will be in your own heart, a heart big enough to hold what peace is: the melody of love, the calmness of an approving conscience, the serenity of a single faith, the composure of courage, the tranquility of self-acceptance, the repose of unselfishness, the harmony of being in tune with self.

Peace, heart of mine; no longer sigh to wander,
Lose not thy life in fruitless quest.
There are no happy islands over yonder;
Come home and rest.

—Henry Van Dyke

I will both lay me down in peace, and sleep.—Psalms 4:8

BITTERS AND SWEETS

Blessed is he who sugar-coats the bitter he must swallow. Each must take a certain amount of bitters or famish. For our world is not all sweet.

Reality requires us to take a little of the bad with the good. This is true of a friend — none is faultless. True of a mate — no two people are always in complete accord. True of a job — none is a paradise. True of a school — all err. True of a church — while this word stirs a hallowed thought, it is made up of humans who are not yet prepared to don halos.

So, don't pass up the sweets because there are bitters; mix them and then swallow.

They saw the glory of the world displayed;
They saw the bitter of it, and the sweet.

—Ernest Dowson
1867 - 1900

But to the hungry soul every bitter thing is sweet.—Proverbs 27:7

DESERVE A GOOD NAME

A good name is not enough — you ought to merit it. Reputation is what people think you are, or think you are not; but character is what you are. A person can gain a good name by publicly denouncing crime while he privately practices it. Stealing secretly and giving openly will cause the world to applaud, but the doer knows he is a fraud.

When a man was asked how much he treasured his name, he replied, placing his hand over his heart, "Not half as much as what I have right here." He was more concerned with being than with seeming.

> *I hate the man who builds his name*
> *On ruins of another's fame.*
>
> *—John Gay*
> 1688 - 1732

Thou hast a name that thou livest, and art dead.—Revelation 3:1

LAUGHTER PROTECTS

When a little boy on his scooter hit a bump in the sidewalk and took a tumble, he paused and then burst out laughing.

A passer-by who saw no fun in the bruises asked: "What's so funny? Why laugh about it?"

The boy replied, "Mr., I'm laughing so I won't cry."

Occasionally we adults hit a rough place in life and suffer a spill; now that is a good time to laugh, lest we lose self-possession. Laughing is a safety-valve which lets off the tensions of irritations; if the valve doesn't work, we become as grim as an owl, but without his proverbial wisdom.

> *Our sincerest laughter*
> *With some pain is fraught;*
> *Our sweetest songs are those that tell of*
> *saddest thought.*
>
> —*Percy Bysshe Shelley*
> 1792 - 1822

Even in laughter the heart is sorrowful.
— Proverbs 14:13

BLESSED ARE THE MERCIFUL

There is no plainer badge of nobility than mercy. It is the formation of so many princely traits. Like the rainbow, it sparkles with many colors: clemency, compassion, forgiveness, pity, yearning. It's one of the measurements of a person; his size is in proportion to his compassion.

If experience makes the man, then it makes mercy more merciful. The need of compassion we have felt in ourselves is more easily extended to others. If we have worn nail-piercing shoes, we are more sympathetic toward him who limps. And an awareness that unrelenting justice would down us all, inclines us toward more clemency for other offenders.

My friend, judge not me,
Thou seest I judge not thee.
Betwixt the stirrup and the ground
Mercy I asked, and mercy found.

—*William Camden*
1551 - 1623

Blessed are the merciful; for they shall obtain mercy.—Matthew 5:8

ENRICHED BY GIVING

Giving is better than receiving, though it is contrary to popular belief. Of course, receiving is good; if not, giving is not good, for you can't have one without the other. But of the two, giving is much more rewarding.

Julius Caesar is reputed to have said that no music was so charming in his ears as the requests of his friends, and the supplications of those in want of his assistance.

A giving hand is a gathering hand — collects more than it hands out. It is most ennobling. It is the life of love. It is humanity's touch of divinity in one word.

Give! as the morning that flows out of heaven;
Give! as the waves when their channel is riven;
Give! as the free air and sunshine are given;
Lavishly, utterly, joyfully give!

—Anonymous

It is more blessed to give than to receive.
— Acts 20:35

THE GIVER WITH THE GIFT

Who gives himself, with his gift, gives the most —life to life. All other giving is small.

Gifts! gifts! how we love them! If they come as gifts — not deceits; if they express goodness — not bribes; if they are free acts of thoughtfulness — not attached to gain-seeking strings and hidden motives.

If you have a message, you can say it with a gift; and it will keep speaking, unless you prove unkind. Remember — the gift and the giver belong together; not good, if detached. So, for the highest type of giving, be and remain the better part of what you give.

For, to the noble mind
Rich gifts wax poor when givers prove unkind.

—*William Shakespeare*
1564 - 1616

A gift is as a precious stone in the eyes of him that hath it: whithersoever it turn-eth, it prospereth.—Proverbs 17:8

NOT SKIN DEEP

The fairest beauty is that which no camera can catch. When beauty is only skin deep, others can see beneath the surface. Outward beauty intoxicates the eye, but inward beauty grabs the heart.

The comeliness which catches the eye can be deceptive, a pretty body with an ugly heart. External handsomeness is the package nature provides, but internal handsomeness is the contents man develops; only a few can have the former, but there is no excuse for anyone's not having the latter. And concerning values, it is a poor product when the container is worth more than the filling.

Handsome is that handsome does.

—*Oliver Goldsmith*
1728 - 1774

Thou ... hast made thy beauty to be abhorred.
—Ezekiel 16:25

MONEY GETS ATTENTION

Money does not make one more winsome — just more welcome. For "the love of money is the root of" much attention to those who have it. Health is more valuable than wealth, but the sick rich man gets more invitations. A request for his presence, however, may be only to reach for his purse, and those doors money opens may slam him on the way out — after his pockets are picked.

Therefore, if you have only thirty coins, watch that Judas kiss — its lips have a taste for silver. And don't be fooled by a little homage; for where money is god, the servants bow.

Prosperity makes friends, adversity tries them.

—Publius Syrus
1st Century B. C.

Wealth maketh many friends... — Proverbs 19:4

LOVE CHANGES THE LOOKS

Nothing gives the world a new look like love. The oceans are bluer, the grass greener, the flowers sweeter, the moon brighter, and even the old grouch down the street seems nicer.

The world has its tragedies and comedies, and because of love, its beauty and brotherhood.

Love gives us something sweet when we are threatened with bitters, a light brighter than the sun when other lights fade, a wealth richer than Solomon when bankruptcy threatens, an ointment for the heart when earth's darts pierce it, a helping hand when we falter.

It is the magic of beauty, the spring of goodness, the bond of closeness.

For love, all love of other sights controls,
And makes one little room, an everywhere.

—*John Donne*
1572 - 1631

And above all these things put on charity [love], which is the bond of perfectness.
— Colossians 3:14

WISELY SILENT

There are so many instances when well-timed silence is better than speech:

— When you don't know what to say.
— When you don't know how to say it.
— When others don't care to hear it.
— When talking would hurt another.
— When you may later regret it.
— When calumny is to be answered best.
— When the heart is so heavy that speech seems
— When suffering prefers to remain mute.
  light.
— When saying nothing is the grandest eloquence.
— When quietude is most persuasive.

Remember — the stars shine in silence, and so can man.

Let thy speech be better than silence, or be silent.
                    —Dionysius the Elder
                    430 - 367 B. C.

But Jesus gave him no answer.   — John 19:9

DEVELOP GOOD HABITS

Today is mine provided my habits let me possess it. For habits not only make the day, they make the man.

Habit eventually becomes character; for what you do and repeat becomes you — and your days. Spontaneous action for the right makes one an ideal person. Accordingly, no life is prepared for a role unbefitting its second nature.

Habits are the avenues through which man largely moves, but not every street leads to where he should go. So, choose with care your destiny, and then through consistent usage, establish a set of habits that will take you on your way.

Nothing is stronger than habit.

—Ovid
19 B. C. - 54 A. D.

And, as his custom was, he went into the synagogue on the sabbath day.—Luke 4:16

THE CALL FOR MEN

Give us men. Good men. Men with true faith, strong minds, heroic hearts and ready hands. Men whose feet have a way of sticking to the path of duty. Men who are as hard as a rock and as soft as a flower. Men who are as steady in their pursuits as the sun is in the heavens. Honest men to whom bribes have no appeal. Men who have a will, who refuse to be putty, shaped and fashioned by the world's fancy. Men who are willing to stand up and be counted; who though the odds are against them still stand. Because they are men.

Let men see, let them know, a real man,
who lives as he was meant to live.

—*Marcus Aurelius*

I will send thee a man out of the land of Benjamin.—I Samuel 9:16

WHOLEHEARTED PRAYING

You must put your heart in prayer, if prayer would put heart in you. Your prayers, whether in public or in private, should be heart-felt expressions to God. Just open your heart and let the sincerity and simplicity of what's there come forth.

The main thing is not the arithmetic of prayers — how numerous they are; nor the range of prayers — how long they are; nor the linguistics of prayers — how grammatical they are; nor the rhetoric of prayers — how eloquent they are; nor the music of prayers — how sweet the voice is; nor the posture of prayers — how the body poses. The chief factor is the heart.

Two went to pray? Better to say
One went to brag, the other to pray.

—Richard Crashaw
1613 - 1649

I cried with my whole heart; hear me, O Lord: I will keep thy statutes.—Psalms 119:145

CLIMB YOUR MOUNTAIN

Some circumstances are more fortuitous than others, but you don't have to be born on a mountain top to get there. You do have to climb and climb judiciously. On the way up, you may be struck by the "arrows of an outrageous fortune," but you can pull out the darts today and they will heal tomorrow.

Principally, man becomes a child of fortune through his own mind and hands; because brain and brawn can work together for his betterment, for the conquering of opposing forces. Hereby he climbs his mountain, and on top he raises the walls for his good luck house.

> *The brave man carves out his fortune, and*
> *every man is the son of his own works.*
>
> *—Miguel de Cervantes*
> 1547 - 1616

Thou art a great people, and hath great power: thou shalt not have one lot only: But the mountain shall be thine.—Joshua 17:17, 18

BETTER TRUST ALL THAN NONE

You may lose occasionally in trusting too many, but you will lose more in trusting too few. For the workings of society are but a trust, without which you won't fit.

While a few prove false, the majority will compensate. There is more to gain in standing with those who are so good they think nobody is bad than to stand with those who are so bad they think nobody is good.

The wiser practice, however, is to be discriminatory with a leaning toward trust, without which you are held suspect; for the eyes and ears of suspicion may largely be seeing and hearing self.

It is more ignominious to mistrust our friends than to be deceived by them.

—*La Rochefoucauld*
1613 - 1680

And Achish believed David.—I Samuel 27:12

SELFISHNESS HINDERS RECEIVING

What do I get out of it? That is the question coming from the self-centered person. Want the answer? Not much! The reason — it will keep one from giving much, and in return the world will reciprocate sparingly. No one can get much from self-centeredness, for it is littleness — a big interest in a little object.

You can't go far, if you are tied to self. Self-absorption forges the chains which so bind a person to his own unhappiness, cynicism and defeat that he is left bound — but not gagged — while the world passes him by.

> *O I could go through all life's troubles singing,*
>   *Turning earth's night to day,*
> *If self were not so fast around me clinging,*
>   *To all I do or say.*
>
> —*Frederick William Faber*
>   1814 - 1863

. . . not seeing mine own profit, but the profit of many . . .—I Corinthians 10:33

BE WARY OF TOO GOOD A BARGAIN

I learned one of the most useful lessons of my life when I was a child — to be cautious of unreasonable bargains. I bought some apples at a greatly reduced price. They looked good, but what I didn't see was all the worms within. I was swindled by the hope of getting something for nothing. Having been relieved of my little cash, I resolved that if I had more sense than a green apple I would from that day proceed in life with more inspection.

Nothing worthwhile in business, education, politics or religion comes free. About all we get free is air — and it is polluted.

You get what you pay for.

—*Gabriel Biel*
1425 - 1495

The king's merchants received the linen yarn at a price.—I Kings 10:28

HONESTY LENDS HONOR

An old English farmer, leaving his sons a small inheritance, wrote in his will: "There is not a dishonest shilling in the whole of it." All had come through honest toil and honest dealings. He was a man of honor inside and out. His integrity had given him more joy than his wealth.

Nothing in life will bring much genuine satisfaction unless one has honor and self-respect.

It was in this vein that James A. Garfield said: "There is one man whose respect I must have at all hazards, and his name is James A. Garfield — for I must room with him, walk with him, work with him, eat with him, commune with him — live with him."

Honor and shame from no condition rise;
Act well your part, there all the honor lies.

—Alexander Pope
1688 - 1744

A gracious woman retaineth honor.
— Proverbs 11:16

A LITTLE FOR THE RAINY DAY

It is exceedingly wise to live within your income. Economy gives an independence not afforded otherwise. One way to have a mint is to practice thrift, for a dollar saved is a dollar made. It is much harder to spend money discretely than to earn it; and harder still to leave some unspent. "Live within your means" is a good motto; but still a better one is, "Save something today, for it may rain tomorrow."

While it is true that there will be no pockets in your shroud, it is just as true that it will take somebody's money to buy one.

Ere you consult your fancy, consult your purse.

—Benjamin Franklin
1706 - 1790

For which of you, intending to build a tower, sitteth not down first, and counteth the cost, whether he have sufficient to finish it?—Luke 14:28

BE A CANDLE

It is gratifying to be just a little candle. Human beams shine far, and if they shine far, they shine near. The darker the night, the brighter they shine, though quietly. Don't mistake the silence of light; it is effective without noise. A candle blows no horn, just shines; do that, and the world will blow a horn for you.

As nobody knows where light goes when it goes out, nobody knows a good deed's whereabouts — except that it does not end. This is one way to be immortal — just be a light.

How far that little candle throws his beams!
So shines a good deed in a naughty world.

—*William Shakespeare*
1564 - 1616

For thou wilt light my candle: the Lord my God will enlighten my darkness.
—Psalms 18:28

WHEN CHURCH SEEMS COLD

If the church seems cold, move to the front. There is more warmth in the "Amen corner" than in Z-row. If your religion is frozen, it is from your own ice.

Remember — if the preacher in the pulpit acts like a dead man, it may be because the pews are filled with corpses.

Come alive, even if it does shock the preacher. Hear the sermon — don't just sit there. Pray—don't just bow. Think. Meditate. Examine yourself. Be friendly — don't stand back and wait to be greeted. And in speaking of the church, start saying "we" —not "they."

> *Converting the church house into an ice house is not a proper conversion.*
>
> *—Anonymous*

My heart was hot within me; while I was musing the fire burned.—Psalms 39:3

UPS AND DOWNS OF LIFE

Life is uneven. It has its ups and downs. There are days of exaltation and there are days of despair. The weather is mixed with sunshine and shadow. Some days are too short, others too long. There are valleys to traverse and mountains to climb. Sailing some seas is smooth, others choppy. Hoeing some rows is easy, others hard.

But in spite of all this, it is a good day when you can crawl out of bed, put on your clothes, go to the table and eat, make an honest living and be a friend to man. That day is yours.

The rose and the thorn, and sorrow and gladness are linked together.

—Muslih-ud-Din Saadi
1184 (?) - 1291

For, lo, the winter is past, the rain is over and gone; the flowers appear on the earth.
— Song of Solomon 2:11, 12

TO RECTIFY IS HUMAN

If "to err is human," then to correct is human. Deity has no need to make amends, for He errs not. However, as a human it is no disgrace to be what you are: fallible man. But as a maker of mistakes, you should be a corrector of them. Error accompanies the struggles of man, and redressing them is the science of human improvement.

If there is anything that needs rectifying, do it; seek pardon; close a breach; make retribution. If your blunder cannot be redressed, at least you can make it right with God and yourself, and then you should forget it.

Things past redress are now with me past care.

—*William Shakespeare*
1564 - 1616

If fire break out, and catch in thorns, so that the stacks of corn, or the standing corn, or the field, be consumed therewith; he that kindleth the fire shall surely make restitution.—Exodus 22:6

SLANDER'S COMBINE

Which is worse? A slanderous tongue or slanderous ears? Since like tongue is welcome only in like ears, then why ask which is worse: the wicked guest or the wicked host?

In grading thieves, there is little choice. And stealing another's reputation is not a job for a lone robber. The name-filcher has to have help in this most benighted thievery, which robs the victim without enriching the spoilers. The malign tongue wags in vain unless there are defaming ears to listen, and vice versa.

> *Who steals my purse steals trash; 'tis*
> *something, nothing;*
> *'Twas mine, 'tis his, and has been slave*
> *to thousands;*
> *But he that filches from me my good name*
> *Robs me of that which not enriches him,*
> *And makes me poor indeed.*

> —*William Shakespeare*
> 1564 - 1616

And they that seek my hurt speak mischievous things, and imagine deceits all the day long.
— Psalms 38:12

BE THANKFUL

"How gloomy you look," said one bucket to another as they were being carried to a well.

"Ah!" replied the second bucket, "I was thinking how useless all this is; for no matter how full we go away, we always come back empty."

Then the first bucket commented: "What a strange way to look at it. I have always been thankful and happy that, however empty we come, we always go away full."

Both were filled alike. The difference was in them. What kind of a bucket are you?

An easy thing, O Power Divine,
To thank thee for these gifts of Thine,
For summer's sunshine, winter's snow,
For hearts that kindle, thoughts that glow;
But when shall I attain to this —
To thank Thee for the things I miss?

—Thomas Wentworth Higginson

. . . my cup runneth over.—Psalms 23:5

BLESSINGS AND REVERSES

Every person has many blessings and at least a few misfortunes. The ones he reflects upon will either strengthen or weaken him.

Our most necessary blessings are apt to be uncounted, because they are the most common: sunshine, rain, oxygen, soil, plants, animals, and a thousand other workings of nature.

The universality of so many blessings, however, does not lower their value. If this commonness tempts us to be ungrateful, let us ask: Where would we stand if the earth caved in? What would we breathe if the oxygen ran out? What would we do if the water dried up?

Reflect upon your present blessings, of which every man has many—not on your past misfortunes, of which all men have some.

—*Charles Dickens*
1812 - 1870

Every good and every perfect gift is from above, and cometh down from the Father of lights.—James 1:17

TRUST

Trust is a quality of life which makes today mine. If I doubt, I lose it.

It is better to have a cupboard empty of food than a heart empty of trust. Empty living is often due to a lack of expectancy. Some people work and pray (?), but don't expect very much.

The food will digest better today, if we trust God for more tomorrow. Floods, droughts, pestilences, but man survives; so obviously it's not impractical to trust. You can better take the strain of life, if you add trust to your food and rest. Whatever man does, it needs an additive — trust.

On God for all events depend;
You cannot want when God's your friend.
Weigh well your part and do your best;
Leave to your Maker all the rest.

—*Nathaniel Cotton*
1705 - 1788

Thou preparest a table before me in the presence of mine enemies; thou anointest my head with oil; my cup runneth over.— Psalms 23:5

DOES MY FAITH LOOK UP?

Faith in divinity strengthens. As a young American preacher, Ray Palmer, sat in his little room meditating on his problems, suddenly, impulsively he began to write, "My Faith Looks Up to Thee." Quickly, he finished the hymn which has inspired millions.

A few years later Dr. Lowell Mason, the great song writer, requested Palmer to contribute a song to a book he was publishing. Palmer remembered this one and presented it to Mason for publication.

Subsequently, the two men met again. "Mr. Palmer," said Mason, "you may live a long time and you may do many great things, but you will be known to posterity as the man who wrote *My Faith Looks Up to Thee.*

> *My faith looks up to thee,*
> *Thou Lamb of Calvary,*
> *Savior Divine*
> *Now hear me while I pray;*
> *Take all my guilt away;*
> *O let me from this day be wholly Thine.*
>
> —*Ray Palmer*
> written 1830

And this is the victory that overcometh the world, even our faith.—I John 5:4

AVAIL YOURSELF OF PRAYER

Many times we cannot get the courage to stand on our feet until we get on our knees. In addition to the divine assistance, prayer helps us gather our inner resources which afford strength.

It is in this sacred experience that man, stripped of deceit and vanity (for there is no point in trying to fool himself or God), may in his unfeigned stature honestly discuss and earnestly petition help for his frailties and faults, trials and troubles, aims and ambitions.

A pouring out of the deepest and truest feelings, a communication of spirit with Spirit, that is what it is. And that is praying.

Lord, till I reach that blissful shore,
No privilege so dear shall be
As thus my inmost soul to pour
In prayer to thee.

—*Charlotte Elliott*

Men ought always to pray, and not to faint.—Luke 18:1

LOVE BINDS

No rope or cable on earth can bind as fast as a single thread of love. It fastens like a lock and is as strong as steel. No one can know its might unless he has been on one end of the strand. It is too strong for any mortal to describe — except in one word: God, for "God is Love."

It is the golden thread which binds heart to heart: the irresistible, unseen force that draws people together, you to me and me to you. It is the world's most unifying quality, which makes each a part of all.

The sweetest lives are those to duty wed,
Whose deeds both great and small,
Are close knit strands of an unbroken thread,
Where love ennobles all.

—Anonymous

That their hearts might be comforted, being knit together in love, and unto all riches of the full assurance of understanding.— Colossians 2:2

KEEP SELF-RESPECT

There is one person whose approbation is worth more than all others. That one is you! As long as you keep his respect, the ill reports of others can't permanently hurt you; but lose it, and all the good that may be said of you is of little help.

What you think of yourself is most important. There is great strength in keeping clean and maintaining self-respect. It will clothe you with an armor your detractors cannot pierce. If you are ever hurt beneath the skin, you will have to do it.

None but one can harm you,
None but yourself who are your greatest foe;
He that respects himself is safe from others,
He wears a coat of mail that none can pierce.

--Henry Wadsworth Longfellow
1807 - 1882

The righteous also shall hold on his way, and he that hath clean hands shall be stronger and stronger.—Job 17:9

GRAB THE PRESENT

Don't postpone living. Don't let life pass you by while you only endure the present. Don't wait for the children to grow up — have a big time while they do. Don't wait until you get that new house — a new outlook is more urgent. Don't wait until all the debts are paid — you might have more later. Don't wait for retirement — then you might be tired.

He who waits may find it a little late. Every day has its reasons to hold up the zest, but just one is needed to go ahead: life's uncertainty. You are passing through only once; so grab all the bliss you can.

> *Act—act in the living Present!*
> *Heart within, and God o'erhead!*
>
> *—Henry Wadsworth Longfellow*
> 1807 - 1882

Are not my days few? cease then, and let me alone, that I may take comfort a little before I go whence I shall not return.
—Job 10:20, 21

DECIDE

Make decisions, make them as wisely as you can, but make them. The fate of life begins with choice, and it is your fate and your prerogative to call the turns that determine it.

He who won't decide has already decided—against success and happiness. It is better to make some bad decisions than to continuously make the worst one of all—no decision.

Weigh the *pros* and *cons*. Get all the expert help you can, but reserve the right to decide. Standing up to life is like being a patient when doctors disagree; you have to make the final judgment.

> *When you have to make a choice and don't make it, that is in itself a choice.*
>
> —*William James*

> So shall thy judgment be; thyself hast decided it.—I Kings 20:40

I WILL DO IT

It is easy to say, "Somebody ought to do that." But the way to get the job done is to say, "I'm going to do that." My being smart enough to see what should be done is a pretty good sign that I'm big enough to do it.

I should take the initiative. It won't do any good to visualize an oak unless I plant an acorn. I must take action. Move. Nevertheless, I should be deliberate, not "rush in where angels dare to tread"; but where angels lead, I should walk in with my eyes open and my sleeves rolled up.

Vision, action, accomplishment, this is the pattern of fortune.

There is a tide in the affairs of men,
Which, taken at the flood, leads on to fortune.

—*William Shakespeare*
1564 - 1616

Then said I, Here am I; send me.—Isaiah 6:8

LINKED TO OTHERS

One of man's supreme needs is a link with others. He craves the closeness and happiness of association. He finds assistance in wholesome companions. They can bear his sorrow and share his joys. They can steady him when he wobbles. They can lift him up when he falls. They can sit beside him when he is sick. They can play with him when he is well.

You want this bond of helpfulness, you say. All right. The method of obtaining it is simple — love people. Love will fasten you to one end of the link.

True love's the gift which God has given
To man alone beneath the heaven;
* * *
It is the secret sympathy,
The silver link, the silken tie,
Which heart to heart and mind to mind
In body and in soul can bind.

—*Sir Walter Scott*
1771 - 1832

The soul of Jonathan was knit with the soul of David, and Jonathan loved him as his own soul.—I Samuel 18:1

TRUTH WINS

Don't fight truth. You can't win. What sometimes is judged victory is premature. Truth won't fall dead in the streets; what appears to be its corpse is only its pounded form dragged into an alley; but look — there it comes again, as straight and strong and unconquerable as ever. No need to try to bury it, for it has inherent resurrection powers and shall rise again.

Of course, truth is harsh. And sometimes it goes a-begging; but when beggars beg no more, it shall still be handing out its favors. So, line up with truth for truth's sake. And for your sake! It's a winner!

It fortifies my soul to know
That, though I perish, Truth is so:
That, howsoe'er I stray and range,
Whate'er I do, Thou dost not change.

—*Arthur Hugh Clough*
1819 - 1861

I have chosen the way of truth.—Psalms 119:30

WISDOM OF KINDNESS

"I'll shape you," said the hammer to a piece of iron as his blows fell upon it. But every blow dulled the edge more and more.

"Let me change you," said the saw as he ripped into the cold metal. However, after losing several teeth, the saw had to quit.

Next, the little flame gently said, "Let me try." And it warmly embraced the iron, and there it stayed until the hardness melted. The forging was then an easy task.

There are hearts like this. They resist blows and cuttings, but soften under the warmth of kindness.

What wisdom can you find that is greater than kindness?
—Jean Jacques Rousseau
1712 - 1778

... and in her tongue is the law of kindness.
—Proverbs 31:26

REVENGE DIGS ITS OWN GRAVE

Revenge may look like justice, but is just self, wounded self, recoiling. Revenge is a fighter, but a dumb one! For as it knifes at the jugular vein of a victim, it slits its own throat. It cannot see far, that its naughty work shall plague itself.

It is the way of strife; for when grievance is revenged, there is a perpetual quarrel. Thus, it is fitting that we ask: When we are wronged, are we going to be gentlemen or savages? Or worse still, are we going to be animals, dog eat dog? Answer that and you will go far in deciding your future.

Let us forget and forgive injuries.

—Miguel de Cervantes
1547 - 1616

Whoso diggeth a pit shall fall therein.—
Proverbs 22:16

HEAR BOTH SIDES

Don't you think you should hear the other side? It just might be possible that you heard the wrong report. If you listened to only one version, you may not have heard the whole story, the whole truth. If you consider all the facts, impartially, you might be tempted to take the other side.

The trouble is, it requires less effort to be hasty than correct; and it is easier to take sides, right or wrong, where sympathies lie. But one truth is crystal clear: judgments should never be formed on either half facts or personal preferences.

Never judge till you've heard the other side.

—Euripides
480 - 406 B.C.

I do the more cheerfully answer for myself.—Acts 24:10

BE CLEMENT

Be slow about marking people off your list. Mercy in your own heart makes the wounds more tolerable. There is too much good in the worst of the worst and too much bad in the best of the best for us to be unforgiving.

If you are mistreated, rise above it. If others condemn you, be magnanimous. If others are little, be big. If there is a tug-of-war, let your end of the rope be charity.

Remember, the cat and the kindness you give away always come back to you. You win by acting bigger than little people.

> *He wanted a bout;*
> *He left me out.*
> *I wanted to win;*
> *I let him in.*
>
> *—Anonymous*

Though I speak with the tongues of men and of angels, and have not charity, I am become as sounding brass, or a tinkling cymbal.—I Corinthians 13:1

SEEK PEACE

Peace is positive. Something to seek. And when it is sought, it is apt to be found, for most people respond in the manner you treat them.

Peace is the tolerance of faults, the willingness to give a little, the triumph of principles, the unselfish pursuit of right which is stronger than might.

The peacemaker has a reconstructed view of life which puts the time and talent of conflict to a better cause. He does more than put up the sword — he beats it into a plowshare. He does more than lay aside the spear — he forges it into a pruning hook. He overcomes evil with good.

Peace, peace is what I seek, and public calm;
Endless extinction of unhappy hates.

—Matthew Arnold
1822 - 1888

Follow peace with all men.—Hebrews 12:14

GOOD SENSE HAS GOOD MANNERS

Good manners and good sense go together. Uncivility reflects on one's thinking. If like manners produce like reactions, then the impolite person sorely has not thought through the consequences of his boorishness.

Good manners will make you welcome, for they put people at ease, allowing others to see your good will. It is the gentleman's way of doing things — not the kicks of a donkey, not the growls of a dog. Courtesy is the refinement which makes human relations run smoothly, without which there is friction.

One thing you can do, even if you are broke, is to be civil; though it costs nothing, it is friends in hand and food on the table.

Some people's manners would shock a monkey.
—American Adage

And Julius courteously entreated Paul.—
Acts 27:3

MIND YOUR OWN BUSINESS

One way to be successful and happy is to mind your own business — not another's. A basic human right is that every person's affairs be inviolate, unless he is infringing on the rights of others.

Meddling is as unhelpful and dangerous as taking a dog by the ears — you don't help him, and you may get bitten. Being a busybody won't make you any friends, but will help you to become better acquainted with some people; in extreme cases, the ambulance driver.

So — what is helpfulness? It is not to snoop about and stick your nose where it doesn't belong!

> *To be idle is a curse,*
> *But to be a busybody is a whole lot worse.*
>
> *—Anonymous*

> But let none of you suffer...as a busybody in other men's matters. —I Peter 4:15

ONE-STRING HARPING

It's a pity to get on a topic and can't get off. Harping on the same string is an imposition on another person's time and ears. The identical tune gets monotonous, and in time will vex the most patient listener. There is no quicker way to cause the welcome mat to shrink. The squeak of the hinges on the man's door as you exit is sweeter to him than your one-string harping.

Enough is enough! And the kindest thing we can say is that it is a plentiful lack of good judgment. That others may enjoy you, learn to play more than one tune.

Harp so on the same string.

—*Miguel De Cervantes*
1547 - 1616

A continual dropping in a very rainy day and a contentious woman are alike. —Proverbs 27:15

PAIN IS IN THE PLAN

Pain! pain! how you visit us mortals! And why? That's the question heard from a million voices around the globe. Why? Why? For the ache of man grants no exemptions, only some forms and sources of it. Sooner or later it strikes all.

So — evidently there are some needs for suffering in the wise plan of the Gracious Designer; for instance: a motivation for action, a teacher of character, a giver of wider dimensions, and a developer of sympathy. Besides these contributory factors, there is another reason for bracing up: pain is short lived, and when it is past, it no longer hurts.

> *Pain dies quickly, and lets her weary prisoners go; the fiercest agonies have shortest reign.*
>
> —*William Cullen Bryant*
> 1794 - 1878

But his flesh upon him shall have pain, and his soul within him shall mourn.—Job 14:22

LOYALTY BEGINS AT HOME

The first requirement of loyalty to others is loyalty to self. The man who reams out himself to suit everybody cuts away until there is nothing left but an empty shell.

All of us know such make-believe people. And just as a fountain cannot flow from nothing, neither can fidelity spring from a void; that which bubbles forth is only pretension.

The true-to-self man is out-and-out honest, truthful, trustworthy, sincere and constant. Where these attributes prevail, no one need fear betrayal; for it would be like tearing off an arm, the pulling away a part of self.

This above all: to thine own self be true,
And it must follow, as the night the day,
Thou canst not then be false to any man.

—*William Shakespeare*
1564 - 1616

I gave my brother Hanani ... charge over Jerusalem: for he was a faithful man ...
—Nehemiah 7:2

CAN'T COUNT AGE BY YEARS

The young in heart. This phrase has fallen upon our ears for years, long enough to make us either old or young: old if we count birthdays; young if we count feelings. This is true because age defies chronology.

If you would count age, then go to the mind and there use the gauges. Measure the dreams, hopes and ambitions. If these qualities are there in abundance, so is your youth — the dawn of renewed quests with the dawn of each new day — though the years be many.

Age does not count as long as there is something else to count. The pursuing never gets old — just tottery.

> *Thou shalt not rob me, thievish Time,*
> *Of all my blessings or my joy;*
> *I have some jewels in my heart*
> *Which thou art powerless to destroy.*
>
> —*Charles Mackay*
> 1814 - 1889

And thine age shall be clearer than the noonday; thou shalt shine forth, thou shalt be as the morning.
—Job 11:17

LEAVE HIM TO HIS CONSCIENCE

It is better to leave an offender to the condemnation of his own conscience than to take vengeance. Fighting him may only make him feel better by giving him a sense of justification. It is more effective to let the pricks spring from his own bosom than for you to hurt him.

By refusing to retaliate, you can maintain a feeling void of offense and save your own heart from a dagger of guilt. Then you can sleep better, work better, play better and pray better. The second wrong never rights the first one, just adds another injury to a world already groaning in guilt.

Leave her to heaven
And to those thorns that in her bosom lodge,
To prick and sting her.

—*William Shakespeare*
1564 - 1616

And they said one to another, we are verily guilty concerning our brother, in that we saw the anguish of his soul, when he besought us, and we would not hear.—Genesis 42:21

THE BEST RULERSHIP

Self-control is the most essential and accomplished form of rulership. Every man's mind can be a throne. And there he can reign, and there he ought to reign.

However, it is a big job, too big for little people. Only the giants in determination can be king of self. The Pygmies in spirit abdicate in favor of people, things and circumstances.

The power of self-preservation is found in self-control. He who loses it becomes a helpless, passive creature with no means of protection. He is as vulnerable as an ancient city with broken down walls.

He who reigns within himself, and rules passions, desires, and fears, is more than a king.

—John Milton
1608 - 1674

He that hath no rule over his own spirit is like a city that is broken down, and without walls.
—Proverbs 25:28

JEALOUSY

Tame jealousy and you will protect yourself from the rage of man; from the misery which knows no peace; from the suspicion which suspects and suspects and suspects; from the provocation which creates its own strife; from the vengeance which never spares itself; from a cruelty as cold as the grave; from the coals of fire which burn from the artless bungling which feeds and fattens on less and less art; from the fear of losing, which drives away what it would keep; and, worst of all, from the affliction which seems never to end.

The venom clamours of a jealous woman
Poison more deadly than a mad dog's tooth.

—*William Shakespeare*
1564 - 1616

For jealousy is the rage of a man: therefore he will not spare in the day of vengeance.
—Proverbs 6:34

December 20

NO RICHES LIKE CONTENTMENT

Contentment is the richest riches this poor, troubled world has ever known, richer than any king's golden, bejeweled crown.

It is easier to find, if we keep in mind the best things are the nearest: pulse in your veins, sight in your eyes, hearing in your ears, food in your stomach, flowers in your yard, water in your well, employment for your mind and hands, friends in your heart, and the path of God for your feet.

Life's plain, common things provide peace, joy and sleep; and if they do not, neither would the state, position or riches one wishes for.

My crown is in my heart, not on my head;
Not decked with diamonds and Indian Stones,
Nor to be seen. My crown is called content.
A crown it is that seldom kings enjoy.

—William Shakespeare
1564 - 1616

But godliness with contentment is great gain.—I Timothy 6:6

LEARN FROM YOUR FOLLY

At times, all have played the fool, but there is a difference: wise fools and stupid fools. The sagacious fool learns from his folly; the thickheaded fool never does. If you can avoid the same blunder, there is hope for you. After all, the world doesn't like the man who never makes a mistake; neither is it fond of the person who keeps on committing the same ones.

Hence, take courage: get up from your fall, wipe off the dust and be thankful — not for the slip, not for the bruises, but that you are now a little smarter.

> *Folly in all of every age we see,*
> *The only difference lies in the degree.*
>
> —*Nicholas Boileau-Despreaux*
> 1636 - 1711

... I have played the fool, and have erred exceedingly. —I Samuel 26:21

BIBLE — RICHEST LITERATURE

The Bible contains the richest and rarest literature of the world. It appeals to the intellectual and aesthetic as well as to the spiritual and moral faculties. It marks the literature of the scholar just like it colors the speech of the street.

John Ruskin considered the Bible "the grandest group of writings extant in the rational world."

The most brilliant passages of Macaulay's writings are rounded with Scripture quotations.

Pope saturated his classics with quotations from Isaiah.

Cowper's "Task" drew much of its imagery from the Scriptures.

Bryant's "Thanatopsis" could never have been written but for the pages of Job.

And myriads of other authors would never have done so excellently without the Bible.

And, weary seekers of the best,
We come back laden from our quest
To find that all the sages said
Is in the Book our mothers read.

—John Greenleaf Whittier
1807 - 1892

For what saith the Scripture? —Romans 4:3

JESUS CHRIST

While men may differ on many points about Jesus Christ, they are agreed that his fame has no rival, that his grip on human hearts has no equal, that his word is sharper than any sword, and that his power to command is mightier than any general.

To his followers, Christ is "the way, the truth, and the life," the Paragon of Goodness, the Model of Morality, and the Savior of the Lost. After nineteen centuries his footprints still glow with a radiant helpfulness, and all who are guided by them lift their own feet of clay to victories over self.

I ask them whence their victory came:
They, with united breath,
Ascribe their conquest to the Lamb,
Their triumph to his death.

—*Isaac Watts*
1674 - 1748

Christ also suffered for us, leaving us an example, that ye should follow his steps.
—I Peter 2:21

December 24

NEED MORE THAN A MERE MAN

We admire the heroism of Napoleon, the dauntlessness of Caesar, the fortitude of Stonewall Jackson. But would a man call for a Napoleon when his wife lies a corpse, or seek the consolation of a Caesar when he buries his child, or send for a Jackson as he prays at the dying bedside of his mother? No! He feels the need of a man possessed with more than courage. He craves the aid of a man of sympathy and kindness, a man acquainted with grief, a man whose words can heal a heart that aches and breaks —a man like Jesus!

Alexander, Caesar, Charlemagne and I myself have founded empires; but upon what do these creations of our genius depend? Upon force. Jesus alone founded His empire upon love, and to this very day millions would die for him.

—*Napoleon Bonaparte*
1769 - 1821

A man of sorrows, and acquainted with grief.
—Isaiah 53:3

ANNO DOMINI

A. D. — in the year of our Lord. And while we know not the day he was born, we know he was. How great the influence of that lowly carpenter. So much that men began to reckon time by his coming, and now no one can date a letter without acknowledging his birth.

Yet he never did the things which ordinarily accompany renown, like go to college, write a book, lead a military force, head a government; but he is recognized as the Master Teacher, author of the New Testament, Commander of the mightiest army, King of Kings; and though he was the object of strife, he is celebrated as the Prince of Peace.

> *The sages and heroes of history are receding from us, and history contracts the record of their deeds into a narrower page. But time has no power over the name and deeds and words of Jesus Christ.*
>
> *—William Ellery Channing*

> For unto us a child is born . . . and his name shall be called Wonderful, Counselor, The Mighty God, The Everlasting Father, The Prince of Peace.—Isaiah 9:6

YOUR HEART IS YOUR WELL

The wellspring of success is man's heart. The lessons of biography clearly teach that the greats of history had internal resources from which they drew as they faced their times.

In letting down our buckets and pulling them up, what do we get? Sparkling, fresh, life-renewing strength? Or empty buckets from wells that are dry? When we need extra faith, more courage, stiller calmness, additional self-approval, more magnanimity, surer steadfastness, and cast down the bucket, do we get the renewal to carry on? Or do we just get older drawing up nothing?

Dig your well deep enough to hit water before you get thirsty.

> *...dropping buckets into empty wells*
> *And growing old in drawing up nothing.*
>
> —*William Cowper*
> 1731 - 1800

These are wells without water. —II Peter 2:17

DO RIGHT

Right is not something just to verbalize on; it is something to be and do. And the steps are simple: know right, believe right and do right. This will give one the basis to hope for attainment, because it is always linked with right.

No person should expect success unless he is right, for it cannot come from wrong; if it does, it is not success — only disguised failure. As quinine is not the makings of a cake, neither are bitter attitudes the ingredients of a sweet life. No wrong road leads to the right place.

Consequently, if wrong, get right; if right, stay right.

If I am right, Thy grace impart,
Still in the right to stay;
If I am wrong; O teach my heart
To find the better way.

—*Alexander Pope*
1688 - 1744

For thou hast done right... —Nehemiah 9:33

TIME BETTER JUDGES SUCCESS

Who succeeds? Not every one who makes history. Many historic characters have failed. Success is not a throne to sit on; it is being king over self. That gives man a kingdom.

Time passes a better judgment on success than the present. Time has a way of lowering the exalted and exalting the lowered. Nineteen centuries ago the Roman Emperor Nero beheaded the Apostle Paul. Nero did the worst he would and was hailed a success; Paul did the best he could and was scorned a failure. But look now. Nero lives in infamy. Paul lives in glory.

Fail I alone, in words and deeds?
Why, all men strive, and who succeeds?

—Robert Browning
1812 - 1889

And if a man also strive for masteries, yet is he not crowned, except he strive lawfully.—II Timothy 2:5

NO TURNING BACK

On and *On* are the success twins. They deserve greatness, for there is no greater ability than stability — steadiness in pursuits.

Apply, Endure and Conquer are the three strings which wrap up the package of life.

Nothing is impossible to men of constant purpose. In every aspect of life, perseverance rules. Pressing on solves our problems, while turning back brings on more. It's the man who presses on that pushes past the crowd. He finds success where drop-outs find failure. The secret is in a disciplined mind and a strong will that won't give up.

> *Know your own bone; gnaw at it, bury it, unearth it, and gnaw it still.*
>
> —*Henry David Thoreau*
> 1817 - 1862

No man, having put his hand to the plow, and looking back, is fit for the kingdom of God.—Luke 9:62

PLAY TO THE LAST

Winning life's game depends on the closing moments. You have to play it well to the conclusion. Nobody wins by running up a high score in the first, second and third quarters, then failing in the fourth. It's the last quarter that determines the score, and the chief importance of the first three is their bearing on the fourth. Don't think you have won just because you are ahead at the quarter or the half.

It is good to start well, but that is not enough. Be sure you go out in a blaze of victory. It's the way you play at the end that counts.

> *Let no one till his death*
> *Be called unhappy. Measure not the work*
> *Until the day's out and the labor done:*
> *Then bring your gauges.*
>
> —*Elizabeth Barrett Browning*
> 1806 - 1861

I have fought a good fight, I have finished my course, I have kept the faith. —II Timothy 4:7

MY FUTURE?

What does the future hold? Much of the past, for history has a way of repeating itself. We handled the past and we can do even better in the future, for hindsight can give us a little foresight, not specifically but generally.

The best thing about the future is that it comes upon us by degrees, a day at a time. We can manage that much.

Whatever it holds, my future is mine: if it be fair weather, let me bask in the sun; if it be storms, let me bend with the wind.

The future belongs to those who can make adjustments.

> *My past is gone; my present is passing; my future is arriving.*
>
> *—Anonymous*

Sanctify yourselves against to-morrow.
—Numbers 11:18

INDEX

— A —

— B —

— C —

— D —

— E —

— F —

— G —

— H —

— I —

— J —

— R —

— S —